THE CURIOUS BIRD LOVER'S HANDBOOK

Writing under a variety of *noms de plume*, **Niall Edworthy** has written over thirty books covering a wide range of subjects: military history, biography, crime, natural history, humour and sport. Niall spent ten years working for the wire agencies AFP and Reuters and currently lives in Sussex with his family.

THE CURIOUS BIRD LOVER'S HANDBOOK

Niall Edworthy

BLACK SWAN

TRANSWORLD PUBLISHERS
61–63 Uxbridge Road, London W5 5SA
www.penguin.co.uk

Transworld is part of the Penguin Random House group of companies
whose addresses can be found at global.penguinrandomhouse.com

Penguin
Random House
UK

First published as *Bald Coot and Screaming Loon* in Great Britain in 2009
by Eden Project Books
an imprint of Transworld Publishers
This edition published as *The Curious Bird Lover's Handbook* by Black Swan in 2017

A CIP catalogue record for this book
is available from the British Library.

ISBN
9781784162719

Typeset in Adobe Garamond and Frutiger
Design by AB3 Design.

Printed and bound by Clays Ltd, Bungay, Suffolk.

Penguin Random House is committed to a sustainable
future for our business, our readers and our planet. This book
is made from Forest Stewardship Council® certified paper.

MIX
Paper from
responsible sources
FSC® C018179

9 10

To my godchildren,
Hope Farquhar
and
Charlie Barnett

Among those [bird lovers] I know of are a Prime Minister, a President, three Secretaries of State, a charwoman, two policemen, two Kings, two Royal Dukes, one Prince, one Princess, a Communist, seven Labour, one Liberal, six Conservative Members of Parliament, several farm-labourers earning ninety shillings a week, a rich man who earns two or three times more than that every hour of the day, at least forty-six schoolmasters, an engine-driver, a postman, and an upholsterer.

**BRITISH ORNITHOLOGIST, NATURALIST, BROADCASTER AND AUTHOR
JAMES FISHER (1912–70)**

I hope you love birds, too. It is economical. It saves going to Heaven.

US POET EMILY DICKINSON (1830–86)

CONTENTS

Foreword   xi

Dinosaurs in Disguise?: How birds came to be   1

The Cloaca Monologues: Courtship and breeding   13

A Cracking Start: Raising the family   27

Love and War: Why birds sing and call   46

Why Don't Birds Wee?: Birds and their bodies   60

A Complex Relationship: Birds and man   84

The Majesty of Flight: How and why birds fly   112

Pole to Pole Without a Map: The mystery of migration   127

Just Behave: The remarkable behaviour of birds   144

Bird Brain: Instinct or intelligence?   162

The Battle to Survive: How birds are coping in a damaged world   173

References and acknowledgements   203

Index   205

FOREWORD

'*WHAT? BIRDS? WHY ME? What have I done wrong?*' An author growls at his publisher at his peril, but that's exactly what I did about a dozen years ago when invited to write a book about birds. Under a *nom de plume*, I had just finished writing the story of an action-packed war operation and the adrenaline was still coursing. The prospect of boning up on the nesting habits of robins made my eyelids sink. It was true that I had become increasingly interested in nature since moving from the city to the South Downs; I had started gardening, I had bought some binoculars, I had hung feeders in the garden and, yes, birds are great – but a book about them! Please, do me a favour!

Luckily, I had the ace up my sleeve and I played it artfully: 'But I am not a scientist, I don't know the first thing about birds beyond that they have feathers, they lay eggs, they go to the loo on my wind-screen, they fly a lot and you can roast some of them. I like them, sure, but . . .'

But I was trumped. 'That, Niall, is exactly why we want someone like you to write the book. We want fresh, innocent eyes on the subject, someone to convey the sense of wonder from their discoveries . . .'

Luckily again, I was rescued by the offer of a separate project and I wriggled out of the trap, but when that was finished, back flew the woodpecking publisher, drilling away at my reluctance. This time, I came without a struggle. A seed of curiosity, planted by the original invitation, had taken root. By then I had *two* sets of binoculars, one upstairs and one down – and I could tell the difference between a blackbird and a goldfinch. I still knew nothing, or very little, about the subject – a vast and varied one – but I was hooked and I was hungry for more knowledge.

A year later, holding the freshly printed first edition in my hand and feeling very proud, I was twittering and chirping my thanks and my apologies. I can't say I wear my binoculars in bed these days, but I am borderline fanatical about birds. My wife's not, nor are my children but that's because they have never read this book – yet! And that's the point about birds in a nutshell – or perhaps any subject. I used to have no interest in birds precisely because I knew absolutely nothing about them, but the more I learned about their extraordinary story – the evolution from dinosaurs (highly probable), behaviour, courtship and family life (remarkable), the mystery of migration (ridiculous), building a nest (you try it), the magic of flight (don't try it!), man's relationship with birds (hang your head), their survival in a world damaged so severely and so rapidly (hang your head lower) – the greater the charm and the fascination. Knowledge – I have a bit of it now, thanks to this book, and I have a love of

birds and nature that I could never have anticipated and will stay with me and grow forever, a wonderful retreat from all the rest. Knowledge of our world, and thanks to it perhaps a dash of wisdom – surely, that's the key to it all, certainly worth a go at any rate. What's the worst that can happen for giving up half a day for a glimpse of an amazing other world?

This book, I hope, contains pretty well everything the man on the Clapham omnibus needs to know about birds. I have tried my best to write it in an accessible and entertaining fashion, sprinkling anecdotes, quotes, sayings and poems amongst the hard facts, translating the more complex science into the readily understandable. I have presented the story of birds in a way that does not oblige you to read the book from cover to cover. Look upon it as a bird feeding table, just fly in and help yourself to some morsels when the hunger for some knowledge takes you. Writing it has made me very happy; I hope I can pass on a little of that happiness to you.

Niall Edworthy, West Sussex, 2016

Dinosaurs in Disguise?

--- HOW BIRDS CAME TO BE

Are birds really descended from dinosaurs?

The answer is somewhere between very probably and almost certainly, yet there is still some debate because the evidence about how and when birds evolved is not conclusive. To some ornithologists, on the other hand, the mystery is not whether birds are descended from dinosaurs but whether they *are* dinosaurs.

The bird–dinosaur debate began with the discovery in 1860 of a fossil in a limestone quarry in Bavaria that astounded the scientific community of the day. The 145-million-year-old fossil is a crow-sized skeleton covered in feathers and it has been so well preserved that even from a picture you can see that the creature was part bird, part reptile. It was dubbed 'Archaeopteryx', meaning ancient wing, and it is considered to be one of the most important fossil finds ever. The feathers, which are unique to birds, are obvious but the skeleton is very unbird-like with its long bony tail, teeth in place of a beak and claws on the wings, giving it a strong resemblance to the running lizard dinosaurs. If there had been no feathers with Archaeopteryx, it would have been wrongly classified as a small dinosaur, just as five previous finds had been. One was displayed in a museum as a running lizard dinosaur for decades before it was realized it was in fact Archaeopteryx.

The majority of ornithologists contending that birds are descended from dinosaurs point out that the two classes of creature share almost 100 physical characteristics, which is far more evidence than they would need to prove their case in a court of law. And in the last 15 years or so, archaeologists have unearthed even more evidence,

~~~~~~~~~

I once had a sparrow alight upon my shoulder for a moment, while I was hoeing in a village garden, and I felt that I was more distinguished by that circumstance than I should have been by any epaulet I could have worn.

US NATURALIST AND WRITER
HENRY DAVID THOREAU
(1817–62)

~~~~~~~~~

including dinosaurs with bird-like features and primitive birds with dinosaur-like features.

The evidence, in both living birds and fossils, to support the theory that birds have evolved from two-legged, running dinosaurs is highly convincing, but it doesn't quite clinch the argument. There are still gaps in the fossil record and other small pockets of doubt that the sceptics, like woodpeckers to a tree trunk, cling on to for the time being – if for no other reason than the sake of a good scientific quarrel. They believe that birds evolved from four-legged reptiles that lived in trees, insisting that any similarity between birds and dinosaurs is an example of convergent evolution, whereby two distinct, unrelated groups of creature coincidentally grow to resemble each other because they happen to live in similar environments.

Why not fur or scales like the rest of us?

Among the many characteristics that birds share with their putative dinosaur ancestors and with present-day reptiles, one of the most telling about their genetic relationship is a protein called keratin. The scaly skin of a reptile and the feathers of a bird are both composed of this robust fibrous compound, which strongly suggests that the latter evolved from the former. What's more, birds still have scales on the lower parts of their legs and feet. The theory is that dinosaurs (or other reptiles) with frayed scales may have had a genetic advantage because they were able to trap air and thus keep warmer than the reptiles with standard scales, which had to wait for the sun to climb high into the sky to warm themselves by lying in its rays. The frayed scales, which slowly grew in length into feathers, helped conserve their owners' energy, enabling the creatures to get to food sources first in the early morning. The sunbathers, meanwhile, will have been weaker in the morning and more sluggish in the ensuing scrap for food. Some of these latter species probably died out while their frayed and feathered cousins moved onwards and upwards.

> **Taking Archaeopteryx as the first bird, scientists estimate that a minimum of 150,000 to 175,000 different species of birds have existed throughout history, though some put the figure as high as 1.5 million. There are approximately 10,000 species alive today.**

There are other advantages to plumage that will have added even greater selective pressure: feathers gave birds camouflage and features to display during courtship, and above all the ability to fly.

Taking the Evolutionary Express

Scientists are constantly amazed by the speed at which birds have mutated into a new form to suit an environment. Incontrovertible proof of this can be seen on the Galapagos Islands, which emerged from the Pacific Ocean floor to the west of Ecuador following a volcanic eruption roughly five million years ago (a short time in evolutionary terms). Birds began to arrive not long afterwards and, without any predators there to worry about, they quickly settled into a cosy existence, gorging on the abundant fish to be found around the islands and doing what they're programmed to do, namely reproducing to continue their genetic line, as efficiently and actively as possible. The islands' cormorants no longer needed wings and over time they grew shorter and shorter as the creatures evolved into the flightless birds we see there today.

The Archaeopteryx's Song

I am only half out of this rock of scales.
What good is armour when you want to fly?
My tail is like a stony pedestal
and not a rudder. If I sit back on it
I sniff winds, clouds, rains, fogs where
I'd be, where I'd be flying, be flying high.
Dinosaurs are spicks and
all I see when I look back
is tardy turdy bonehead swamps
whose scruples are dumb tons.
Damnable plates and plaques
Can't even keep out ticks.
They think when they make the ground thunder
as they lumber for a horn-lock or a rut
that someone is afraid, that everyone is afraid,
but no one is afraid. The lords of creation
are in my mate's next egg's next egg's next egg,
stegosaur. It's feathers I need, more feathers
for the life to come. And these iron teeth
I want away, and a smooth beak
to cut the air. And these claws
on my wings, what use are they
except to drag me down, do you imagine
I am ever going to crawl again?
When I first left that crag
and flapped low and heavy over the ravine
I saw past present and future
like a dying tyrannosaur

and skimmed it with a hiss.
I will teach my sons and daughters to live
on mist and fire and fly to the stars.

SCOTTISH POET EDWIN MORGAN (1920–)

Evolution just a doddle

To many people, the feral pigeon, a familiar sight waddling along the pavements and squares of our cities and towns, is an ugly, unhygienic bird, a 'rat with wings' that should be shunned or even exterminated. But even its many detractors would have to acknowledge that the bird is one of the most successful species on the planet, with a rare ability to adapt with great speed to new environments and thereby ensure its survival – indeed increase. Such is its adaptability that the only place in the world where you won't find the feral

pigeon is on the polar icecaps. It has colonized everywhere else, which is no mean achievement for a species whose natural habitat was a rocky coastline until man began to domesticate the bird about the time of William the Conqueror. Since then, the birds have slowly moved into our towns where the food is plentiful and where the buildings provide similar, but much warmer homes than wind-blasted cliffs. No relation of the wood pigeon that nests in trees, the 'feral' descended from the rock dove, but it is now extremely rare to find them living on our coastlines. Most creatures take hundreds of thousands, even millions of years to leave one environment and adapt to another, but the unfancied feral pigeon has done it in under a millennium. So next time you walk past a 'feral' as it plucks some cold French fries out of a bin, raise your hat and give it a nod of respect.

The raven and the dove are the first birds to be mentioned by name in the Bible:

Then it came about at the end of forty days, that Noah opened the window of the ark which he had made; And he sent out a raven, and it flew here and there until the water was dried up from the earth. Then he sent out a dove from him, to see if the water was abated from the face of the land; But the dove found no resting place for the sole of her foot, so she returned to him into the ark, for the water was on the surface of all the earth. Then he put out his hand and took her, and brought her into the ark to himself. So he waited yet another seven days; and again he sent out the dove from the ark. The dove came to him toward evening, and behold, in her beak was a freshly picked olive leaf. So Noah knew that the water was abated from the earth. Then he waited yet another seven days, and sent out the dove; but she did not return to him again.

Genesis 8:6–12

~~~~~~~~~~~~~~~~~~~~~~~~~~

I value my garden more for being full of blackbirds than cherries, and very frankly give them fruit for their songs.

ENGLISH ESSAYIST JOSEPH ADDISON (1672–1719)

~~~~~~~~~~~~~~~~~~~~~~~~~~

❝ A turkey is more occult and awful than all the angels and archangels. In so far as God has partly revealed to us an angelic world, he has partly told us what an angel means. But God has never told us what a turkey means. And if you go and stare at a live turkey for an hour or two, you will find by the end of it that the enigma has rather increased than diminished. ❞

ENGLISH WRITER G. K. CHESTERTON (1874–1936)

Beastly Business

Bestiaries, popular in Europe in the Middle Ages, were books containing elaborate illustrations, descriptions of animals and often moral lessons to be drawn from their behaviour. Below are extracts from a bestiary from http://bestiary.ca

THE PARROT IS A BIRD *found in India that can be taught to speak like a man. It learns better when it is young, but if it will not learn one must hit it over the head with an iron bar. It can say 'ave' by nature, but must be taught all other words. Its beak is so hard that if the parrot falls from a height it can break its fall with its beak. Parrots are coloured green with a purple-red collar; they hate the rain because the water makes their colours appear ugly. There are two kinds of parrot: the kind with three toes have a mean disposition, but the ones with six toes are gentle.*

THE OWL HAUNTS RUINS *and flies only at night; preferring to live in darkness it hides from the light. It is a dirty, slothful bird that pollutes its own nest with its dung. It is often found near tombs and lives in caves. Some say it flies backwards. When other birds see it hiding during the day, they noisily attack it to betray its hiding place. Owls cry out when they sense that someone is about to die.*

THE NIGHTINGALE HAS A SWEET SONG, *and loves to sing. It sings to relieve the tedium as it sits on its nest through the night. At dawn it sings so enthusiastically that it almost dies. Sometimes nightingales compete with each other with their songs, and the one that loses the competition often dies.*

THE HOOPOE *is said to be a filthy bird that collects human dung and builds its nest with it, and eats bad-smelling excrement. It also likes to live around tombs. It is further said*

that if the blood of the hoopoe is rubbed on a sleeping man, devils will try to strangle him.

AT NIGHT, CRANES
take turns keeping watch
for enemies. The one who
is on duty holds a stone
up with one claw; if
the watcher falls asleep
the stone will fall and
wake him. If the
wind is strong cranes
swallow sand or carry
stones for ballast.
Cranes are the enemy of
pygmies, with whom they
are constantly at war.

THE FLESH OF THE PEACOCK *is so hard that it does not rot, and can hardly be cooked in fire or digested by the liver. Its voice is terrible, causing fear in the listener when the bird unexpectedly begins to cry out. Its head is like a snake, its breast is sapphire-coloured, it has red feathers in its wings, and has a long green tail adorned with eyes. If it receives praise for its beauty, it raises its tail, leaving its rear parts bare. When it suddenly awakes it cries out, because it thinks its beauty has been lost. It is a bird with great foresight. Its feet are very ugly, so the peacock refuses to fly high in order to keep its feet hidden.*

AS YOUNG PELICANS GROW, *they begin to strike their parents in the face with their beaks. Though the pelican has great love for its young, it strikes back and kills them. After three days, the mother pierces her side or her breast and lets her blood fall on the dead birds, and thus revives them. Some say it is the male pelican that kills the young and revives them with his blood.*

A rare old bird indeed

The kiwi is a mighty queer creature, a fine example of how evolution will quickly dump some characteristics and replace them with others if left undisturbed for a few million years. Once upon a time, the ancestors of this endangered nocturnal bird could fly perfectly well, but today it has more in common with a hedgehog than with its feathered cousins. Found only in New Zealand, where it is strictly protected by law, this friendly, chicken-sized bird has wings that have been reduced by lack of use to no more than two-inch feathered stumps. In a land with no mammals to prey on it – until man arrived – the kiwi, like its flightless cousins the ostrich and the emu, had no reason to fly. Spending so much time on the ground, it developed an incredible sense of smell, using its long, slender, flexible bill, which has nostrils at the lower end, to forage for insects, grubs and worms on the forest floor – just as a pig or a hedgehog does.

Unlike its moa cousins and countless other species of New Zealand birds, the kiwi managed to survive the twin onslaught of man and his land mammals for two main reasons. First, it is highly alert to possible danger and although it may look ungainly it can outrun a human being. Then, if it does fail to escape its predator, it can

Numbers of different creature species

Amphibians	6,000
Reptiles	8,000
Birds	10,000
Fish	30,000
Insects	Countless millions

deliver a flesh-tearing blow with its sharp, three-toed feet that will make even the hungriest or most determined interloper think twice about having a second go.

Why the ostrich gave up flying

All animals are programmed to expend as little energy as possible, so if a local ecology presents a bird with the chance of giving up on the exhausting business of flight it will take it with open wings. All flightless birds such as the kiwi, emu, rhea and cassowary retain all the major physical features to indicate that their ancestors once flew the skies, but over time, exploiting the favourable conditions on the ground, they adapted to a life on their feet, sprouting long powerful legs to make up for their inability to escape from predators by taking to the air. At full pelt, an ostrich can reach speeds of 80km/h and they could outrun most athletes for more than 20 minutes.

The ostrich is the tallest and heaviest bird in the world and its flightless cousins, with the exception of the kiwi, are huge too, but if they could still fly, they would be a fraction of their gargantuan size. The ostrich is to the wren what an elephant is to a pygmy mouse and its scale is key to its evolutionary success because it serves as a deterrent in itself. The ostrich weighs between 8 and 12 times more than the kori bustard, the world's heaviest flying bird. You'd have to be insensible with drink or stark raving bonkers to fight an ostrich, but if the whim ever took you, be warned that with one kick your feathered opponent could crush your skull, break your spine or rip out your innards.

❛ Let us, before leaving the subject, once more look back across that awesome gulf of 150 million years to the days when Archaeopteryxes hopped about on the shores of the reedy pools in Bavaria. It is hard to conceive so long a time. The mind does not comprehend it. Imagine a line 150 feet long, each foot representing a million years; ourselves a point at this end, Archaeopteryx a point at the other. If we start moving toward the ancient bird, we shall find that by the time we have passed the days of Tut-ankh-amen's great-grandfather, we shall have progressed a distance about equal to the width of a thick pencil-line, or one millimetre to 3333 years. After going back the vast space of a third of an inch we shall have passed far beyond historic times to the early Stone Age of Man, and at the end of an inch we shall be well into Glacial times. The first foot of our 150-foot journey will have brought us only to the beginning of the latest or Pleistocene epoch of earth's history, and we will have accomplished less than half the journey ere we reach the fauna of the Paris basin and the great Diatryma of Eocene days. And even when we at length reach the journey's end, we are still a long way from the starting point of birds. Thus we may realize that geologically speaking a thousand years is not really such a very long time; it is only that our thoughts are small. ❜

GLOVER MORRILL ALLEN (1879–1942), *BIRDS AND THEIR ATTRIBUTES*

The Cloaca Monologues

COURTSHIP AND BREEDING

Why do some birds settle down with partners and others play the field?

It is often said that 90 per cent of birds are monogamous in that a male and female will form a pair bond. A small percentage of birds, generally the larger ones that live longer, such as the swan and the albatross and most birds of prey, do settle down for life. But most animals aren't built to stay faithful to one partner. On the contrary, they are 'hardwired' to put it about as much as possible: the male to spread his genes far and wide, and the female to choose the fittest mate to father and help rear the chicks. Monogamy is a risk that most animals, including birds, cannot afford to take.

Scientists now in fact draw a distinction between sexual monogamy (mating exclusively with one partner during the breeding season) and social monogamy (pairing up with a mate to raise offspring but also having a bit on the side if the opportunity presents). In one famous study, female blackbirds that paired with sterilized males still laid eggs that hatched. So while most birds, including all those in your back garden, like to pop to the hedge next door 'to borrow some berries', 90 per cent of birds are *socially* monogamous. This form of monogamy works for both sexes. The female gets an extra pair of mandibles to help around the home, building the nest, foraging for food, feeding chicks, disposing of waste, maybe even keeping the eggs warm. The male, meanwhile, gets to fulfil his main purpose in life, namely to continue the family line.

The Birds

He. Where thou dwellest, in what grove,
    Tell me Fair One, tell me Love;
    Where thou thy charming nest dost build,
    O thou pride of every field!

She. Yonder stands a lonely tree,
     There I live and mourn for thee;
     Morning drinks my silent tear,
     And evening winds my sorrow bear.

He. O thou summer's harmony,
    I have liv'd and mourn'd for thee;
    Each day I mourn along the wood,
    And night hath heard my sorrows loud.

She. Dost thou truly long for me?
     And am I thus sweet to thee?
     Sorrow now is at an end,
     O my Lover and my Friend!

He. Come, on wings of joy we'll fly
    To where my bower hangs on high;
    Come, and make thy calm retreat
    Among green leaves and blossoms sweet.

ENGLISH POET WILLIAM BLAKE (1757–1827)

How do birds have sex?

This is not a straightforward business: bird breeding is like speed-dating with fighting; Newcastle city centre on a Friday night, only noisier and tougher. For most species, it goes something like this: the male starts staking out his territory in mid-winter, beats up or sees off any rivals that dare enter his patch, puts on his finest plumage (see peacocks) and/or starts to sing as loudly and attractively as he can to alert passing females, and then fixes a date with a mate – or several if he's playing the field. The male really has his work cut out trying to woo the female, because she tends to reject his first few approaches, forcing him to try a bit harder each time until he's almost worn himself out. She needs him to prove his fitness to father her young. Males, especially the feisty robin, sometimes have to fight off rivals for their mate's affection ('You looking at my bird or what?'). If the male succeeds in winning over the female, the next stage of the relationship is to build a nest. For most birds this is a joint enter-prise.

Then, and only then, do the new couple finally get down to cop-ulating – and this part is a very quick affair, surprising perhaps after all that scrapping and prancing about. Blink and you'll miss it. After a bit of awkward fumbling and manoeuvring, the male mounts the female in a flash. Sperm is passed over when the male's cloaca, a hole under his tail also used for excreting, is conjoined with the female's. This is known as a 'cloacal kiss'. The female turns the fertilized ovum into a newlaid egg in just 24 hours. As the female, typically, stores the sperm for days or even weeks, copulation need take place only once, though it may occur several times. Birds of prey, and large waders and shorebirds, will probably produce two eggs, laid two or three days apart; most other birds lay an egg every day, the overall number varying greatly between species. The pair then incubate their clutch for however long it takes (in the case of most garden birds, roughly two weeks). Once the chicks hatch, the parents feed them until they are ready to fledge, making hundreds of trips each day to and from the nest to deliver food. Great tits have been recorded as making over 1,000 trips a day. If you have ever wondered why the birds in your garden look a little tatty and dishevelled towards the end of the summer, now you know. Their offspring have run them ragged.

Once the breeding season is over, the

bird's reproductive organs shrivel up to reduce its weight for flying. The death rate among small garden birds is very high; they are doing well if they survive in their first year of life to experience a single breeding season of their own. In temperate regions like Britain, the peak breeding season is roughly March to June, when food sources for the young, such as caterpillars and flying insects, are most abundant.

Mute swans are one of just a handful of bird species that take a partner for life. The 'divorce rate' among mute swan couples is roughly 5 per cent. (The equivalent figure for the Bewick's swan, a Siberian bird that winters in Britain, is even lower, at less than 1 per cent.) Mutes don't rush into their relationships either; courtship is elaborate and flirtatious, resuming at the start of each breeding season. The courting couple indulge in a theatrical display of affection known as 'head-turning', in which the two birds touch breasts and, inadvertently of course, form the shape of a heart. The male, or cob, is highly protective of his partner, the nest the pair build and the young they produce and it's best to give cobs a wide berth during the breeding season. Swans' parenting behaviour is similar to the traditional human model, with the male as the protector and the female as the nurturer, although the male will 'help around the house' too. Both will look after the cygnets and take them for rides on their backs to keep them safe from predators.

Serial adulterers
Over 50 per cent of reed bunting chicks are not fathered by the pair male but are the result of an adulterous liaison, the highest recorded rate of 'infidelity' among any bird species.

How birds manage to build nests, often highly elaborate ones, is one of nature's greatest miracles. Try making one with your hands using twigs, hair, spittle and moss, and see how far you get. Now try making one with your mouth. The fact that birds can make them using just a beak, often to minute specifications and incredibly intricate designs, is remarkable. Some nests are conspicuously scruffy, such as those of doves, pigeons, house sparrows and crows, but most are elaborate structures built to design specifications unique to their species. Constructing the future family home takes a huge amount of effort and expenditure of energy. Long-tailed tits, for instance, use roughly 2,000 feathers in building a nest and fly over 600 miles to collect all the materials. Spiders are vital to birds in the breeding season as their sticky webs are used by a great number of birds as a glue or mortar for binding together the main construction materials of twigs, moss, grasses, hair and feathers.

And I beheld the birds in the bushes building their nests, which no man, with all his wits, could ever make. And I marvelled to know who taught the magpie to lay the sticks in which to lay her eggs and to breed her young; for no craftsman could make such a nest hold together, and it would be a wonderful mason who could construct a mould for it.

WILLIAM LANGLAND (C. 1330–86), *PIERS PLOWMAN*

The nest of the goldcrest is one of the finest examples of avian engineering skills. Europe's smallest bird needs as much warmth as it can get because it has such a low ratio of body volume to surface area. All birds are vulnerable to the cold because they need to maintain a high body temperature, but the minuscule goldcrest is especially at risk. So, over millions of years, they've learned how to construct highly sophisticated homes for their chicks. Using cobwebs as a kind of suspension rope, the goldcrest hangs its sack-like nest towards the end of a long branch, safe from predators. It also uses cobwebs as the glue for an outer wall made of lichen and moss, which is then lined with layers of feathers, hair and more moss. The breathtaking detail of the design is demonstrated in the entrance, which is situated at the top of the sack under or very close to the branch, which acts almost as a door to keep out the cold. As a finishing touch, the little birds even add a screen or curtain of large feathers around the entrance.

Boring but true

A cousin of the cormorant, the shag has caused much amusement in the back row of the classroom for generations, but the name, by which it has been known since the early Middle Ages, has nothing to do with its reproductive habits. The word refers to the shaggy tuft of plumage that appears on the top of its head in the summer.

The lengths males will go to ...

Male birds often have to go the extra mile – and more – to attract a mate. Songbirds sing until they almost burst with the effort; the male wren builds over a dozen nests for the female to choose from; the tern brings a fish as a love gift; cranes dance together; the peregrine falcon, the world's fastest creature, stages a spectacular aerobatic display; swans go on a protracted date before committing, and the male peacock has – over tens of millions of years – developed the most spectacular fan of tail feathers for the sole purpose of attracting a female. But the grebe conducts the most elaborate and romantic courtship ritual (at least to sentimental, dewy-eyed humans), with male and female meeting breast to breast and then dancing with each other for several days.

Pluck off, pal, she's mine

Contrary to popular belief, it is not the striking colourful plumage of the cock pheasant that sets hens' hearts a-flutter in the breeding season, it's the red, fleshy lobes – or 'wattles' – hanging off his face. When the male is aroused, the wattles inflate, their size telling the female everything she needs to know about his physical well-being, including testosterone levels. Pheasant breeding is a supreme form of selective breeding, regulated not by man but by their own instinctive behaviour, an avian Nazi-style eugenics programme happening right here, on the other side of our hedges. The fittest males attract the most females – which explains why you often see half a dozen of the dull, brown females following one brightly coloured male. They frequently end up all living together in a kind of polygamy. Top males pull all the birds and get to fulfil their raison d'être, to continue their line, leaving the losers to hop about in the undergrowth and wait to get shot by a chinless man in plus fours high on sherry and brandy. The 'loser' birds often hang around other pheasants in the hope of jumping an unsuspecting female when the big, scary stud pheasant with massive wattles is too busy filling his face with grain to notice. But if the capo catches him in the act, a very nasty fight will ensue. Like cockerels, pheasants have sharp spurs on their feet that can cause severe damage; it is at this point that the loser pheasant finds out that nature hasn't just endowed his rival with a superior pair of wattles, but also much bigger spurs.

The strange case of the homosexual necrophiliac duck

In 1995, Dutch researcher Kees Moeliker was sitting in his office in Rotterdam's Natural History Museum when a drake mallard crashed into the clear glass façade of the building and slumped to the ground dead. When Moeliker went outside a few minutes later to inspect the casualty, he was shocked to find another male mallard viciously pecking the back of its head. After a couple of minutes, this drake mounted the corpse and started to copulate furiously, pecking the dead duck's head as he did so. This continued for a full 75 minutes before Moeliker made his presence known, whereupon the necrophiliac drake ceased its morbid humping and waddled off to peck some grass. Moeliker was so astonished by what he had witnessed that he set out to investigate the science behind it, and earned himself the coveted Ig Nobel prize for improbable research in the biology category. Moeliker, now the museum's bird curator, believes the pair were engaged in a 'rape flight attempt': a common phenomenon in the duck world where the male pursues another duck and forces it to mate. 'Rape is a normal reproductive strategy in mallards,' he was reported in the press as saying. 'When one died the other one just went for it and didn't get any negative feedback – well, didn't get any feedback.'

Can a bird be gay?

Homosexuality in animals is a controversial subject. Some people use the ambiguous evidence as proof that same-sex orientation is completely natural, others to show that it is completely not. You stride into the gay bird debate at your peril. To muddy the water still further, the really unhelpful answer to this question is: yes, no, maybe.

Homosexual behaviour, but generally not sex, has been witnessed in a number of bird species. If a male does mount another male as if to copulate, it does so not to enjoy fulfilling sexual relations, as humans

IN THE GARDEN

Granny was wrong; bread is no good

For years people have been leaving out bread for their birds, but the current wisdom suggests we should think of alternatives. It's not that the bread is bad for birds, it just doesn't have much goodness. A bird that fills up on bread will be missing out on more nutritious foods.

might, but for one of a number of other reasons including mistaken identity ('Forgive me, I am SO sorry! From behind you're a dead ringer for my wife . . .'). Sometimes it will be an expression of sexual frustration when a male, after searching high and low, has been unable to find a mate. This is especially common amongst seabirds breeding in colonies in which there happen to be more males than females. There is, however, plenty of evidence of other homosexual behaviour in birds, particularly amongst ducks, geese and swans. Roughly 25 per cent of Australian black swan families are raised by homosexual couples. One or both of two male black swans mate with a female then, once she's laid the eggs, chase her away, incubate the eggs themselves and bring up a family on their own. The good sense behind this evolutionary phenomenon is that two cobs, being a more powerful unit than a cob and a pen, can protect a larger territory and provide their brood with more to eat. Broods raised by a homosexual couple are more likely to survive than those raised by a heterosexual pair.

Roy and Silo, a pair of apparently gay chinstrap penguins in New York's Central Park Zoo, have found themselves at the heart of the animal homosexuality debate in recent years. In 1999, the two started 'going out' and doing all the things that you'd expect a couple of gay penguins to do: vocalizing to one another, shunning female company and mounting each other. After they had unsuccessfully tried to incubate a rock, the chief zookeeper gave them a fertile egg to test their parenting skills. To the delight of American liberals, Roy and Silo successfully raised a female chick called Tango and, to their even greater delight, Tango came of age and promptly waddled off to pair up with another female called Tazuni. The less liberal members of the human community, keeping a watchful monocle on developments at the zoo, grumbled that the homosexual bond only arose because the penguins were in captivity and not in their natural environment. They also pointed out that, in the wild, male chinstraps share the task of incubating the egg with the female, while in other penguin species the male does all the incubating. So, they concluded, there was no big deal about Roy and Silo sitting on a egg. But in 2005 the grumblers swapped popping their monocles for popping champagne corks when the shocking news leaked from the zoo that Silo had walked out on Roy for a hot Californian chick called Scrappy! The new couple made no attempt to hide their love for one another, hanging out by the pool, vocalizing and indulging in some heavy petting, while poor old Roy moped about looking miserable.

~~~~~~~~~~

Use what talents you possess: the woods would be very silent if no birds sang there except those that sang best.

US AUTHOR AND CLERGYMAN
HENRY VAN DYKE (1852–1933)

~~~~~~~~~~

The wandering albatross, a model of fidelity

Most birds pair up with a mate for one breeding season and will grab a bit on the side when the other's not looking, but not so the wandering albatross, the most faithful of all birds, that will stay with its partner for the five or six decades of its life. These remarkable creatures, with the longest wingspan – 11 feet – of any bird, live on the wing for five to seven years after leaving the nest where they were born, on one of the sub-Antarctic islands. Not once do they touch the land as they circumnavigate the globe, skimming the frozen waters of the Southern Ocean from time to time to catch squid, octopus, cuttlefish and the offal thrown overboard by trawlermen. Held aloft by the powerful winds found in high southern latitudes, the wandering albatross can soar for hours without once having to go to the effort of flapping its wings. It will have circled the globe several dozen, even hundreds of times by the time it returns to land to find its lifelong mate. For millions of years, the wandering albatross has been one of the few birds that dies of old age, but today it is far more likely to perish painfully on the baited hooks of an 80-mile-long line from a trawler emptying our oceans of tuna.

The intriguing sex life of the dunnock

The dunnock is a dull, dun, common bird of no obvious distinction that you may see shuffling along the bottom of a hedge or, if it's feeling adventurous, along the edge of a flower bed. It's so unremarkable that it is invariably mistaken for a sparrow. Indeed, for centuries this shy little bird has been more commonly known as a 'hedge sparrow' – but be careful not to use that name if you find yourself standing in the same hedge as a 'bird-nerd', aka a 'twitcher' from the extremist-pedant wing of the birdwatching community. His binoculars will steam up and he will inform you sternly that the dunnock is not, in fact, a member of the sparrow family, but comes from a rather more obscure little group known as Accentors, of which it is the only representative in the UK.

The boring little dunnock, then, is the last bird you'd expect to have a thrilling sex life, but it is in fact something of a goer. If birds had newspapers, dunnocks would rarely be out of the tabloid headlines. In an area with a plentiful supply of food, the male attracts two or three mates, which is unusual enough in itself; but if food is hard to come by it starts to get even more interesting. Worried that the chicks she will produce won't have enough to eat, the female goes in search of a second male to help her bring up the brood. The first mate holds his dominant position and sings his head off to let everyone know he's still top bird in the hedge. Although he will tolerate his mate's 'bit on the side' because he knows the interloper will

help bring up the young, he watches her every move, following her around suspiciously. If the female manages to escape his attention for a moment, she and the second male will hop into the bushes and mate. But the story doesn't end there because the cuckolded partner has developed an extraordinary technique for making sure it is his sperm that wins the day. When he and his mate come to copulate, she lifts her tail to expose her distended cloaca. But instead of immediately rubbing it with his own cloaca, the male pecks hers with his beak, making it throb and expel the interloper's sperm in the form of a droplet. Only then will he mount her. Who'd have thought the hedgerows of Britain's suburbs shivered and shook with such intrigue?

Including seasonal visitors and passers-by, there are over 550 different species of birds in Britain, more than in any other European country.

A Cracking Start

RAISING THE FAMILY

Creating an egg is all in a day's work

The production of a bird egg is a remarkable and rapid business. The male's sperm fertilizes an ovum, or egg, which pushes through the ovary and sets off down the long tube of the oviduct developing, as it goes, the beginnings of the white (aka the albumen) and the yolk, which serves as the food source for the embryo – a source that in many cases is almost exhausted by the time the chick hatches. Three hours later, the egg moves into the uterus where a gland that secretes a lime compound (calcium carbonate mainly) will create the porous shell over the ensuing 20 hours. It is thought that the colours and markings of the eggshell are produced by bile pigments and

> *I'm youth, I'm joy, I'm a little bird that has broken out of the egg.*
> SCOTTISH NOVELIST SIR JAMES BARRIE (1860–1937)

the haemoglobin in blood. Thus it takes a mother bird just one day to create an ideal environment for her embryonic chick and a new life. Eggshells are porous and delicate so that the chicks can absorb oxygen through them and then peck their way out. White eggs are usually laid by birds safe from predators; the coloured, speckled ones

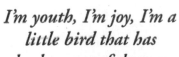

evolved as a camouflage for more vulnerable species. As a general rule, the more conspicuously coloured the egg, the worse it tastes.

Why don't cuckoos lay eggs and raise their own young in their own damned nest?

'These cuckoos, they come over here from Africa, stealing our nests, exploiting our better nature and corrupting our youth. They're just lazy, good-for-nothing parasites . . .' Were there an Alf Garnett-style bigot in the avian community, it would be towards the European cuckoo that he'd direct most of his xenophobic spleen because the cuckoo does exactly that. This elusive dove-sized bird, with the handsome looks of a bird of prey and the song of an angel smoking pot, comes to Britain from Africa in the spring and lays its eggs in the nests of other birds, especially dunnocks, meadow pipits, pied wagtails and reed warblers. The cuckoo chooses these 'foster' birds because their eggs look very similar to her own so she can exploit their parental instincts to bring up her young. Cuckoo chicks always hatch first and they evict the eggs or young of the host bird, which will then feed the cuckoo chick as if it were her own – and all this while her own young lie splattered on the ground below.

The cuckoo is indeed a parasite or, more correctly, a 'brood parasite' and it is only doing what all animals are programmed to do, namely whatever it takes to further the genetic line and produce as many young as it can. By laying her eggs in the nests of other birds, a cuckoo is able to lay many more eggs than she would if she laid them in a nest of her own. And there is another advantage: feeding and raising chicks is

Britain's most common garden birds and their proper names
House sparrow (*Passer domesticus*)
Starling (*Sturnus vulgaris*)
Blackbird (*Turdus merula*)
Blue tit (*Cyanistes caeruleus*)
Chaffinch (*Fringilla coelebs*)
Wood pigeon (*Columba palumbus*)
Collared dove (*Streptopelia decaocto*)
Robin (*Erithacus rubecula*)
Great tit (*Parus major*)
Goldfinch (*Carduelis carduelis*)
(Based on numbers recorded by RSPB Big Garden Birdwatch 2014)

an exhausting business that places a big strain on the parents' energy levels, so why not let some dumb dunnock do the hard graft while you go and play the field? You'd have to be a feathered fool not to.

Parents from hell

European coots make very strict parents. If one of the larger chicks becomes too demanding of food, or hostile towards its siblings, the parent will sometimes pick it up with its beak and give it a good shake, or even submerge it under water. Parental aggression is thought to reduce demands for feedings, giving the smaller chicks a fairer share. It also encourages independence. Occasionally, the admonished chick is so distraught by its rough treatment that it paddles away, never to return. Coots lay up to ten eggs, but only half the chicks – beautifully clothed in jet-black down with heads of bright orange, scarlet and purplish blue – will make it to adulthood.

~~~~~~~~

I hope you love birds, too. It is economical. It saves going to Heaven.

US POET EMILY DICKINSON
(1830–86)

~~~~~~~~

❝ A pair of honey-buzzards . . . built them a large shallow nest, composed of twigs and lined with dead beechen leaves, upon a tall slender beech near the middle of Selborne-hanger, in the summer of 1780. In the middle of the month of June a bold boy climbed this tree, though standing on so steep and dizzy a situation, and brought down an egg, the only one in the nest, which had been sat on for some time, and contained the embrio of a young bird. The egg was smaller, and not so round as those of the common buzzard; was dotted at each end with small red spots, and surrounded in the middle with a broad bloody zone.

The hen-bird was shot, and answered exactly to Mr. Ray's description of that species; had a black cere, short thick legs, and a long tail. When on the wing this species may be easily distinguished from the common buzzard by its hawk-like appearance, small head, wings not so blunt, and longer tail. This specimen contained in its craw some limbs of frogs, and many grey snails without shells. The irides of the eyes of this bird were of a beautiful bright yellow colour.

About the tenth of July in the same summer a pair of sparrow-hawks bred in an old crow's nest on a low beech in the same hanger; and as their brood, which was numerous, began to grow up, became so daring and ravenous, that they were a terror to all the dames in the village that had chickens or ducklings under their care. A boy climbed the tree, and found the young so fledged that they all escaped from him: but discovered that a good house had been kept: the larder was well-stored with provisions; for he brought down a young blackbird, jay, and house martin, all clean picked, and some half devoured. The old birds had been observed to make sad havoc for some days among the new-flown swallows and martins, which, being but lately out of their nests, had not acquired those powers and command of wing that enable them, when more mature, to set such enemies at defiance. ❞

ENGLISH CLERGYMAN AND NATURALIST GILBERT WHITE (1720–93), *NATURAL HISTORY AND ANTIQUITIES OF SELBORNE* (1789)

How to survive on a cold egg for four months

Emperor penguins breed during the coldest time of the year in the Antarctic when the wind-chill factor can send temperatures plunging to –60°C. Only a handful of animals on the planet are able to survive such conditions, let alone rear their young in them, but the penguins pull off this extraordinary feat using a host of tricks with which evolution has endowed them. After the entire colony has waddled up to 70 miles in from the edge of the ice pack, the female lays her egg and transfers it, often with great diffi-

~~~~~~~~

Fall is my favourite season in Los Angeles, watching the birds change colour and fall from the trees.

US TELEVISION PERSONALITY
DAVID LETTERMAN (1947–)

~~~~~~~~

culty, onto the feet of the male, desperately trying not to let it fall onto the ice where it would die in seconds. Handover complete, the female immediately disappears for up to two months in search of food which she will regurgitate for her newly hatched chick on her return. The male is left to incubate the egg which he does by balancing it on his feet and covering it with a feathered 'brood pouch'. Emperor penguins are the sole species of bird where only the male incubates the egg: for two months he just stands there getting battered and frozen by everything the Antarctic winter can throw at him. He is not alone by any means, but surrounded by thousands of other males, all huddling together to keep out the perishing wind. The huge commune slowly revolves and shuffles so that each gets a

IN THE GARDEN

Help birds to nest close to your home

Most birds start to build their nest in early spring in preparation for the breeding season.

Gather up some old **plant matter** from the garden, drying it out if necessary, and leave it in loose piles near hedges and under trees. Long grass, straw, hay, dead flower stems, twigs and small sticks will all be put to use.

Some birds, such as the house sparrow, will also use **fur**, **hair**, **wool** and other soft natural materials.

Don't throw away **fresh green leaves** pruned from shrubs in spring, or **moss** raked from your lawn, as starlings use these for their nests.

House martins, song thrushes and blackbirds need **mud** to construct their nests. The edge of a pond is ideal, but if the weather has been dry you can make your own wet, muddy patch by watering the odd corner of a flower bed.

period in the warmth of the centre. It takes up to three days for the chick to hatch. If it hatches before the mother has returned, the male feeds it a curd-like substance from a gland in his oesophagus. When the females return (usually not later than two weeks after the chicks have hatched), each finds her partner without difficulty in the giant throng by recognizing his unique call. Then the starving males, who haven't eaten since the colony began their retreat to breed almost four months earlier, head off to the sea in search of a richly deserved meal of their own. Thereafter the parents take it in turns to forage and regurgitate food for the chick. When they are two and a half months old, the chicks congregate in a crèche, crowding together for warmth while their parents are hunting.

The Hen

Alas, my Child, where is the Pen
That can do Justice to the Hen?
Like Royalty, She goes her way,
Laying foundations every day,
Though not for Public Buildings, yet
For Custard, Cake and Omelette.
Or if too Old for such a use
They have their Fling at some Abuse,
As when to Censure Plays Unfit
Upon the Stage they make a Hit,
Or at elections Seal the Fate
Of an Obnoxious Candidate.
No wonder, Child, we prize the Hen,
Whose Egg is mightier than the Pen.

US WRITER AND ARTIST OLIVER HERFORD (1863–1935)

Egg facts

- It would take 40 minutes to hard boil an ostrich egg.

- The extinct elephant bird of Madagascar laid the biggest eggs ever, weighing almost two stone.

- The smallest egg of any living bird is that of the bee hummingbird, weighing half a gram – it would take 120 to match the weight of one standard hen's egg.

- The eggs of most garden birds are incubated for between 11 and 15 days.

Doing bird

The endangered great Indian hornbill, a strange-looking creature found in India and southeast Asia, grows up to four feet long and carries a highly distinctive and apparently useless 'casque' of solid ivory on the upper part of its bill. Its breeding behaviour is as odd as its appearance. When the female is ready to lay her eggs, she disappears into a hole in a tree which she seals up with a mixture of droppings, regurgitated food and earth brought by her partner, leaving a small slit through which he can continue to pass food and she can drop out her waste. Safe from predators, she stays in her birthing prison for three or four months until the chicks are well developed. In some species, the female breaks out of the structure earlier, and the chicks seal themselves in again, allowing both parents to forage and pass them food.

The male bower-bird of Australia and New Guinea is one of the most fascinating creatures on the planet. The 'bower' (nest) he builds to attract a female is a masterpiece of decoration, almost human in its artistry, detail and urgency to impress. After constructing a small hut out of twigs and branches, he sets about adorning the interior

Puffin breeding facts

- They nest in burrows, some formerly occupied by rabbits, on clifftops.

- Parents take turns to incubate the one egg laid per season in 32-hour shifts.

- They feed the chick five or six times a day, flying up to 400 miles a day to find fish.

- They carry up to 20 small fish at a go in their colourful beaks when foraging for their chick.

- The parents are so tired (or should that be puffed?) from feeding the chick that they eventually give up, after about 40 days, and hunger forces the youngster to go and earn its own way in the world.

IN THE GARDEN
What to do if you find a baby bird

In late spring and early summer, when chicks are hatching and fledging, it is common to come across a baby bird on the ground. As the chicks grow, one may get accidentally nudged over the edge of the nest: if the one you find is covered in downy feathers, or is in a vulnerable position, such as the road or pavement, then it probably does need help and should be moved to the relative safety of nearby undergrowth. The advice is to put the bird as high up as possible out of the reach of predators, and as close to where you found it as possible so the parents can find and feed it. In the great majority of instances, however, the bird, no matter how terrified and vulnerable it looks, will be absolutely fine if it's left alone. More often than not, it is a fledgling about to take wing for the first time and the last thing it needs is a galumphing, well-meaning human clumsily trying to pick it up. The instinctive reaction of people who care about animals is to take some action, but often the wisest and kindest thing to do is to walk away. It's highly likely that the parents of the bird are very close by and probably even watching with mounting consternation as the caring human passer-by tries to help out. If you're worried that the bird will be taken by a cat or other predator, the advice is to watch over it from a distance and shoo away the interloper.

with colourful objects including flowers, feathers, fruit, shells, berries, stones, glass, plastic and paper. There are 18 species of bower-bird, and two of them, the satin and the regent, use leaves and twigs to paint the interior of the bowers with a dye made from chewed-up plants, charcoal and saliva. The building and decoration can take months and the bird will often move the objects around into different arrangements until he is perfectly happy. When the female tours the area to inspect the efforts of all the local suitors, the male performs a weird dance outside his bower, and in the case of some species will offer her one of his colourful objects as a love gift. Just as some of the dullest-looking birds are the best singers, it is the bower-bird species with the dreariest plumage that builds the most elaborate bowers. It's all about attracting a mate, whether you go in for singing beautifully, dressing up in sensational plumage, or showing off your interior design skills.

Cain and Abel

Most birds of prey lay two eggs, but can feed only one chick adequately; they will favour the first to hatch and effectively abandon the other. The elder sibling tends to bully the younger chick to death and then eat it – all with full parental approval – so that not a scrap of nutrition is wasted.

Coming of age is a leap in the dark

The cliff-dwelling guillemot lays one egg, shaped like a cone so that if it's nudged it's more likely to spin on the spot than roll off the edge. Unlike many birds, the guillemot can recognize its own egg and will return it to the nest if it has been moved. The chick hatches after four or five weeks and remains on the ledge of the cliff for about 16 days, waddling anxiously around and exercising its wings. Then one night the chick comes of age in dramatic fashion. Called by its parents from the water below, the chick leaps into darkness, hopefully tumbling harmlessly off the rocks and into the swelling sea. The parents then escort it further out to sea, feeding, teaching and caring for it, until it can fly and fish for itself. The chicks of the razorbill, the guillemot's cousin in the auk family, perform a similar rite of passage.

Sing a song of sixpence,
A pocket full of rye;
Four-and-twenty blackbirds
Baked in a pie!

When the pie was opened
The birds began to sing;
Was not that a dainty dish
To set before the king?

The king was in his counting-house,
Counting out his money;
The queen was in the parlour,
Eating bread and honey.

The maid was in the garden,
Hanging out the clothes;
When down came a blackbird
And snapped off her nose.

MEDIEVAL NURSERY RHYME

All songbirds emerge from the egg naked and blind. Some may say that that's just plain nidicolous.

Can a swan really break our legs with its wings?

Swans can be very aggressive protecting their young and their territory, especially during the breeding season. Unlike most other animals, swans don't protect a square area but a linear one, a stretch of a lake or river, and woe betide anyone who glides into a cob's path when his cygnets are about. Rival cobs bear the brunt of their belligerence, but as any dog or canoeist will tell you, they're not the only ones at risk of a violent pecking. But the oft-repeated warning that a swan can break a human leg with a swipe of its wings is nonsense. Yes, it will hurt like hell and probably leave a bruise, but there is virtually no chance of it fracturing a healthy dense human bone, protected by flesh, muscle and clothing. The swan's own bones, though tough, are hollow and lightweight, like those of most birds, so that it can fly. A very elderly person with brittle bones, or a very small child, would feel a blow more keenly than others, but a fracture is still highly unlikely.

The stately-sailing swan
Gives out his snowy plumage to the gale;
And, arching proud his neck, with oary feet
Bears forward fierce, and guards his osier isle,
Protective of his young.

SCOTTISH POET JAMES THOMSON (1700–48)

How long can a bird expect to live?

It varies greatly between the species but most birds we see in our gardens will do well to reach their first birthday, the majority falling victim to predators or starvation. Broadly speaking, the larger the bird, the longer the life. Birds of prey, who are rarely preyed upon themselves except by humans, can live for 20 or 30 years; and many seabirds, which have a very low annual death rate of under 10 per cent, will also make it into their twenties. Parrots and albatrosses are the longest-living, often reaching a fifth, sixth or even seventh decade. Waders live between five and 10 years. Garden birds such as robins, sparrows, tits and finches generally have a lifespan of one or two, though in rare cases that can stretch to eight. Roughly 75 per cent of the population of small garden birds dies in the course of every year.

Is there a pecking order in bird communities?

Amongst birds that feed in groups or flocks, like sparrows and some tits, there is a ranking system which is represented in the bird's markings. The older, stronger, more dominant bird gets the best seat at the bird table, while the younger, weaker ones have to scrap for the leftovers. Once the dominant bird has eaten its fill, and moves off to preen itself, copulate or just sit back and enjoy the view from a nearby branch, those that remain at the feeding site are more vulnerable to predators as there are fewer eyes on the lookout. The young and the frail are therefore at greater risk; it is a case of the survival of the strongest. Birds may look cute, but there's not a charitable or altruistic feather on their bodies. Great tits and house sparrows have come to establish their position in the pecking order by displaying their rank, just like soldiers, with stripes of darker feathers: the widest denoting the most senior. What no bird can afford to do if it can help it is waste time fighting over feed, which both burns up valuable energy and distracts the attention from outside dangers. Nature has worked out that there's no point in throwing haymakers in the shrubbery over a couple of grass seeds when Tiddles the cat is on the prowl.

The Thrush's Nest

Within a thick and spreading hawthorn bush
   That overhung a molehill large and round,
I heard from morn to morn a merry thrush
   Sing hymns to sunrise, and I drank the sound
With joy; and, often, an intruding guest,
   I watched her secret toil from day to day –
How true she warped the moss to form a nest,
   And modelled it within with wood and clay;
And by and by, like heath-bells gilt with dew,
   There lay her shining eggs, as bright as flowers,
Ink-spotted over shells of greeny blue;
   And there I witnessed, in the sunny hours,
A brood of nature's minstrels chirp and fly,
   Glad as that sunshine and the laughing sky.

ENGLISH POET JOHN CLARE (1793–1864)

Superlative birds

Smallest: bee hummingbird: 5cm long and weighing between 1.5g and 2g

Heaviest flying bird: kori bustard and great bustard: can weigh upwards of 18kg

Heaviest: ostrich: average weight 90kg–130kg, maximum 156kg

Tallest: ostrich: 1.8m–2.7m

Longest wingspan: wandering albatross: 3.4m or more

Longest bill: Australian pelican: 47cm

Fastest flying: peregrine falcon: 180km/h (when diving)

Slowest: American woodcock: 8km/h

Fastest wingbeat: hummingbird

Longest soaring: albatross and condor

Longest airborne seabird: sooty tern: 3 to 10 years without landing

Longest airborne land bird: swift: 3 years without landing

Longest two-way migration: Arctic tern: 40,200km

Strongest sense of smell: kiwi

Keenest sense of hearing: barn owl

Best eyesight: owls and other birds of prey

Most intelligent: African grey parrot and crow

Most talkative: African grey parrot

Fastest running: ostrich: 70km/h

Fastest underwater swimmer: gentoo penguin: 65km/h

Deepest diver: emperor penguin: 540m

Longest underwater: emperor penguin: 18 minutes

Coldest temperature endured: snowy owl: –62.5°C

Greatest weight-carrying capacity: bald eagle or pallas fish eagle: can lift 6.5kg

Longest without eating: male emperor penguin: 3–4 months when incubating

Most northerly nesting: ivory gull: at edge of Arctic Circle ice sheet

Largest nest: social weavers: 300-chamber 'apartment' nests 8m long and 2m high

Worst-smelling nest: Eurasian hoopoe

Largest egg: ostrich: 18cm by 14cm

Largest clutch by a nidicolous (born naked and blind) species: blue tit: 19 eggs

Largest clutch by a nidifugous (born downy and active) species: bobwhite quail: 28 eggs

Largest average clutch size: grey partridge: 15–19

Smallest clutch: albatross: 1 egg every 2 years

Longest uninterrupted incubation period: emperor penguin: 65 days

Shortest incubation period: small songbirds: 11 days

Longest fledging period of flying birds: wandering albatross: 270 days

Fastest to breeding maturity: common quail: 5 weeks

Slowest to breeding maturity: royal albatross and wandering albatross: 6–10 years

Longest-lived wild bird: albatross: upwards of 60 years

Country with most endangered species: Indonesia: 130

Country with the highest percentage of its species endangered: New Zealand: 30 per cent

RSPB ADVICE ON WHAT FOOD TO OFFER YOUR BIRDS

The better **bird-seed mixtures** contain plenty of flaked maize, sunflower seeds and peanut granules. Mixes containing chunks or whole nuts are suitable for winter feeding only. Small seeds, such as millet, attract mostly house sparrows, dunnocks, finches, reed buntings and collared doves, while flaked maize is taken readily by blackbirds. Tits and greenfinches favour peanuts and sunflower seeds. Pinhead oatmeal is excellent for many birds.

Black sunflower seeds are an excellent all-year food. The oil content is higher in black than in striped ones, which makes them more nutritious. Sunflower hearts are better still because

they are easier to eat, leave no mess and are more hygienic. The birds don't have to break open casings which become a health hazard lying below a feeder covered in disease-riddled waste.

Peanuts are rich in fat and are popular with tits, greenfinches, house sparrows, nuthatches, great spotted woodpeckers and siskins. Crushed or grated nuts attract robins, dunnocks and even wrens. Nuthatches and coal tits may hoard peanuts. Salted or dry-roasted peanuts should not be used.

Fat balls and other fat-based food bars are widely available and make excellent winter food. If they are sold in nylon-mesh bags, always remove the bag before putting the fat ball out – the soft mesh can trap and injure birds.

Mealworms are relished by robins and blue tits and may attract other insect-eating birds such as pied wagtails. They are a natural food and can be used to feed birds throughout the year. Mealworms can be expensive to buy and many people now grow their own. It is very important to make sure the mealworms are fresh as dead or rancid ones can cause salmonella poisoning and other illnesses.

Meaty tinned dog and cat food is a good substitute for earthworms during dry periods when worms are difficult to find. Blackbirds readily take dog food and even feed it to their chicks.

Fermented dairy products such as **cheese** are attractive to robins, wrens and dunnocks. They prefer it grated.

Fresh coconut in the shell. Rinse out any residues of the sweet coconut water from the middle of the coconut before hanging it out, to prevent the build-up of black mildew.

Cooked rice, brown or white (without added salt), is beneficial and readily accepted by all species during severe winter weather. Uncooked rice may be eaten by birds such as pigeons, doves and pheasants but is less likely to attract other species.

Uncooked porridge oats are readily taken by a number of bird species, as is pinhead oatmeal.

Any **breakfast cereal** is acceptable bird food, although you need to be careful to put out only small quantities at a time. It is best offered dry, with a supply of drinking water nearby, since it quickly turns into pulp once wetted.

RSPB ADVICE ON WHAT FOOD *NOT* TO OFFER YOUR BIRDS

Salted foods that birds can't digest and which damage the nervous system.

Some peanuts can be high in a natural poison that can kill birds, so buy from a reputable dealer who will guarantee their nuts don't contain aflatoxin.

Wheat and barley grains are often included in commercial seed mixtures, but they are really only suitable for pigeons, doves and pheasants, which feed on the ground and rapidly increase in numbers, deterring the smaller species.

Avoid seed mixtures that have **split peas**, **beans**, **dried rice** or **lentils** as only the larger species can eat them dry. These are added to some cheaper seed mixes to bulk them up.

Polyunsaturated margarines or vegetable oils: these are unsuitable for birds. Unlike humans, birds need high levels of saturated fat, such as found in raw suet and lard. Moreover the soft fats can easily get smeared onto the feathers, destroying their waterproofing and insulating qualities.

Dry biscuit is not recommended as birds may choke on the hard lumps. It is sometimes added to cheaper seed mixtures for bulk – look out for green or pink lumps, and avoid any mixture containing them. Soaked dog biscuit is excellent, except in hot weather as it quickly dries out. Petfood may attract larger birds such as magpies and gulls, and also neighbourhood cats, so don't use it if that happens.

Never give **milk** to any bird. They're not designed to digest milk, which will cause serious illness and even death.

Desiccated coconut should never be used as it may swell once inside a bird and kill it.

Porridge oats must never be cooked as this makes them glutinous and they may harden around a bird's beak.

Mouldy and stale food: while many moulds are harmless, there are some that can cause respiratory infections in birds, so it is best to be cautious and avoid mouldy food entirely. If food turns mouldy or stale on your bird table, you are probably putting out too large a quantity for the birds to eat in one day. Always remove any decaying food as it provides a breeding ground for salmonella food-poisoning bacteria.

Love and War

WHY BIRDS SING AND CALL

Why do birds sing?
And why is it only the males?

When we lie in bed in the morning as the watery late winter sun seeps through our curtains, the mad chattering of the birds outside tells us that the avian world is alive once again with the frenetic business of breeding. It's the males making most of the noise, prompted by the rising level of testosterone in their bodies, and they have only two things on their mind as they squawk and tweet and chirrup: love and war. The signature song of a male songbird has a twin purpose: to attract a female and to deter a male rival from entering his territory and trying to pull his bird. Females don't need to sing because they're the ones that do the choosing. (Female European robins are an exception to this rule, noisily defending their own territory outside of the breeding season.) Females judge the complexity and quality of his song to weigh up a male's potential fitness as a partner.

You may have noticed that for the second half of the year your garden is a fairly quiet place, compared with the musical maelstrom filling the air for the first six months. That's because our birds don't breed in the autumn and winter, and so there's little reason to sing. Most of the noises birds make at this time are calls, not songs. The breeding season begins in late winter, reaches a noisy climax in May, and peters out in June and July after the chicks have fledged and the exhausted parents can finally ease up a little.

Often each male has characteristic features to his songs so that every individual sounds fractionally different. Each can therefore recognize the songs of his neighbours, who have also settled down with a mate and thus pose no threat. This means he doesn't have to waste valuable energy, at an especially energy-sapping period of the year, erupting into his 'Oi-you!-get-out-of-my-bush-leave-my bird-alone!' routine every time his neighbour has a quick chirrup. It is only when a stranger, an unattached male from another area, turns up that he has to go to the lung-busting effort of warning him off.

The principle holds true for the most part that the plainer the bird, the better it sings. And vice versa, the more colourful the bird, the worse it sings (witness the peacock).

A Bird's Anger

A summer's morning that has but one voice;
Five hundred stooks, like golden lovers, lean
Their heads together, in their quiet way,
And but one bird sings, of a number seen.

It is the lark, that louder, louder sings,
As though but this one thought possessed his mind:
'You silent robin, blackbird, thrush, and finch,
I'll sing enough for all you lazy kind!'

And when I hear him at this daring task,
'Peace, little bird,' I say, 'and take some rest;
Stop that wild, screaming fire of angry song,
Before it makes a coffin of your nest.'

WELSH POET W. H. DAVIES (1871–1940)

What's the difference between a call and a song?

A call is uttered by females as well as males. The ability to call is genetically inherited, not learned. A call is short and to the point, e.g. 'Get the hell out of that bird bath, Socks the cat is about.' A song is more complex, longer and sung only by the males to attract a female mate or warn off rival males from their territory. Many birds that don't sing, such as gulls and parrots, have complex repertoires of calls. All birds can call or make a noise, but it's only the passerines, or songbirds, that sing.

It's *passerine* to you, ducky

'Passerine' refers to birds with three toes pointing forwards and one pointing backwards, but to you and me it is just a fancy word for 'songbird'. If you want to impress someone with your intelligence, say to them, by way of a conversation starter: 'I can't tell you how beautifully the passerines in my garden were vocalizing this morning.' There are over 4,000 passerines, almost half the bird species in the world. All common garden birds are passerines, except for the wood pigeon and collared dove.

World in harmony

Insomniacs may beg to differ, but the dawn chorus is one of the great wonders of nature. It is a sound that has been heard around the world from, well, the dawn of time, and in all environments: European and North American woods, tropical rainforest, African savannahs . . . But quite why songbirds put on such a magnificent choral performance each spring morning before the sun rises is still something of a mystery. For a start, it should be noted that there's little else to do at that time of the day if you're a bird. Foraging for food is not an option as seeds and insects are more difficult to find in the gloom and there is a greater risk of being taken by a predator. (Cats do most of their hunting at dawn and dusk when the light is poor.) As so often with birds, there seems to be more than one explanation. One is that sound travels as much as 20 times more effectively at daybreak since there is little other noise and generally little wind, but the main reason seems to be that the males (who do all the singing) see dawn as a perfect opportunity, in what will soon become a busy day of feeding, preening and cat-dodging, to attract a female. A cold night of sitting in a bush with no food since the evening before greatly depletes a bird's energy reserves. The hearty early morning choristers, all desperately trying to out-sing their love rivals, are thus sending out a statement of their machismo and their fitness as a partner: 'Hey, darling, check *me* out. I may be knackered and freezing but I can still bust a big tune for you.'

Some birds, though, notably the nightingale, have become fed up with all the early morning competition for the airwaves and have evolved the cunning trick of doing most of their singing by night.

> Then from the neighboring thicket the mockingbird,
>   wildest of singers,
> Swinging aloft on a willow spray that hung o'er the water,
> Shook from his little throat such floods of delirious music,
> That the whole air and the woods and the waves seemed
>   silent to listen.

US POET HENRY WADSWORTH LONGFELLOW (1807–82)

Bird song varies enormously, according to habitat. Thrushes, blackbirds, nightingales and other woodland species have rich, loud, complex songs so they can be heard through dense foliage. Birds living in flat marshland, by contrast, have simple, repetitive songs suited to the open, uncluttered surroundings.

Let me be to Thee as the circling bird,
Or bat with tender and air-crisping wings
That shapes in half-light his departing rings,
From both of whom a changeless note is heard.
I have found my music in a common word,
Trying each pleasurable throat that sings
And every praisèd sequence of sweet strings,
And know infallibly which I preferred.

The authentic cadence was discovered late
Which ends those only strains that I approve,
And other science all gone out of date
And minor sweetness scarce made mention of:
I have found the dominant of my range and state –
Love, O my God, to call Thee Love and Love.

ENGLISH POET GERARD MANLEY HOPKINS (1844–89)

Odd fact
The nightingale also
sings during the day.

Birds named after the sound they make

Cuckoo
Chiffchaff
Whipoorwill
Macaw
Hoopoe
Chough
Crake
Kittiwake
Pipit
Shrike
Twite
Whimbrel
Whooper swan

Alwite, me old cock sparrer?

Many species of birds communicate in dialects peculiar to their area. Males do this because a female is more likely to be attracted to a bird familiar with local conditions than any old johnny-fly-by-night passing through. As with human communities, some local dialects are much stronger than others, making them almost unrecognizable to other members of the species from other areas.

❝"An abode without birds is like meat without seasoning." Such was not my abode for I found myself suddenly neighbour to the birds; not by having imprisoned one, but having caged myself near them. I was not only nearer to some of those which commonly frequent the garden and the orchard, but to those wilder and more thrilling songsters of the forest which, rarely, or never serenade a villager. ❞

HENRY DAVID THOREAU, *WALDEN, OR LIFE IN THE WOODS*

Breaking news ...

There is truth in the saying that the early bird catches the worm because song thrushes, robins, blackbirds and skylarks, all of which enjoy a worm for breakfast, are among the earliest risers.

Front row seat

If you want to go outdoors to listen to a dawn chorus in all its glory, rather than one muffled by curtains, walls and earplugs, then check the weather forecast, wait for a fine, clear morning with next to no wind and head into a secluded spot in your garden or beyond to an area with an even larger concentration of songbirds. Late April to early June is the best period, when summer visitors have added their voices to those of the permanent residents. Dawn chorus begins an hour before sunrise, peaks 30 minutes later and ends half an hour after sun-up.

Best singers
Song thrush
Mockingbird
Skylark
Nightingale
Warblers
Blackbird

❝ Though I know something about British birds I should have been lost and confused among American birds, of which unhappily I know little or nothing. Colonel Roosevelt not only knew more about American birds than I did about British birds, but he knew about British birds also. What he had lacked was an opportunity of hearing their songs, and you cannot get a knowledge of the songs of birds in any other way than by listening to them.

… We began our walk, and when a song was heard I told him the name of the bird. I noticed that as soon as I mentioned the name it was unnecessary to tell him more. He knew what the bird was like. It was not necessary for him to see it. He knew the kind of bird it was, its habits and appearance. He just wanted to complete his knowledge by hearing the song. He had, too, a very trained ear for bird songs, which cannot be acquired without having spent much time in listening to them. How he had found time in that busy life to acquire this knowledge so thoroughly it is almost impossible to imagine, but there the knowledge and training undoubtedly were. He had one of the most perfectly trained ears for bird songs that I have ever known, so that if three or four birds were singing together he would pick out their songs, distinguish each, and ask to be told each separate name; and when farther on we heard any bird for a second time, he would remember the song from the first telling and be able to name the bird himself. ❞

SIR EDWARD GREY, BRITISH FOREIGN SECRETARY 1905–16, OF HIS CLOSE FRIEND AND FELLOW BIRD ENTHUSIAST PRESIDENT TEDDY ROOSEVELT

Why does the garden go so quiet at the end of the summer?

At the end of the breeding season, birds are exhausted, dishevelled and in need of a change of scene. Many birds have made tens, even hundreds of thousands of trips in and out of bushes and hedges to feed their chicks, leaving their feathers in need of renewal. When they lose their feathers, they are more vulnerable to predators because they cannot fly so well. While their plumage regenerates, they keep their heads down. Another reason behind their silence is that once the breeding season is over, males no longer need to sing to attract a mate or defend a territory, and the family no longer needs its nest once the chicks have fledged and set out on their own. Late summer and early autumn is also harvest time when food is in abundant supply for birds as well as people, so many birds leave their breeding grounds to enjoy the berries and seeds on offer in farmland, orchards and woods.

~~~~~~~~~~~

The language of birds is very ancient, and, like other ancient modes of speech, very elliptical: little is said, but much is meant.

GILBERT WHITE

~~~~~~~~~~~

I take my joy in the cry of the gannet
And the sound of the curlew
Instead of the laughter of men;
The singing of the gull
Instead of the drinking of mead.

FROM *THE SEAFARER*, OLD ENGLISH POEM, AUTHOR AND DATE UNKNOWN.

The skylark is so universally diffused in these islands, and so abundant, well known and favourite a species, that anything beyond a brief and prosaic account of its habits would appear superfluous. His image, better than any portray it, already exists in every mind. A distinguished ornithologist, writing of the sparrow, declines to describe its language, and asks his reader to open his window and hear it for himself. In like manner, I may ask the reader to listen to the lark's song, which exists registered in his own brain. For he must have heard it times without number, this being a music which, like the rain and sunshine, falls on all of us. If someone, too curious, should desire me not

to concern myself with the images and registered sensations of others' brains, but to record here my own impressions and feelings, I could but refer him to Shelley's 'Ode to a Skylark', which describes the bird at its best – the bird, and the feeling produced on the listener. Some ornithologist (I blush to say it) has pointed out that the poet's description is unscientific and of no value; nevertheless, it embodies what we all feel at times, although we may be without inspiration, and have only dull prose for expression. It is true that there are those who are not moved by nature's sights and sounds, even in her special moments, who regard a skylark merely as something to eat with a delicate flavour. It is well, if we desire to think the best we can of our fellows, to look on such persons as exceptions, like those, perhaps fabled, monsters of antiquity who feasted on nightingales' tongues and other strange meats.

BRITISH NATURALIST AND ORNITHOLOGIST W. H. HUDSON (1841–1922)

To a Skylark

Hail to thee, blithe Spirit!
Bird thou never wert –
That from Heaven or near it
Pourest thy full heart
In profuse strains of unpremeditated art.

Higher still and higher
From the earth thou springest,
Like a cloud of fire;
The blue deep thou wingest,
And singing still dost soar, and soaring ever singest.

In the golden lightning
Of the sunken sun,
O'er which clouds are bright'ning,
Thou dost float and run,
Like an unbodied joy whose race is just begun.

The pale purple even
Melts around thy flight;
Like a star of heaven,
 In the broad daylight
Thou art unseen, but yet I hear thy shrill delight –

Keen as are the arrows
Of that silver sphere
Whose intense lamp narrows
In the white dawn clear,
Until we hardly see, we feel that it is there.

All the earth and air
With thy voice is loud,
As, when night is bare,
From one lonely cloud
The moon rains out her beams, and Heaven is overflow'ed.

What thou art we know not;
What is most like thee?
From rainbow clouds there flow not
Drops so bright to see,
As from thy presence showers a rain of melody: –

Like a poet hidden
In the light of thought,
Singing hymns unbidden,
Till the world is wrought
To sympathy with hopes and fears it heeded not:

Like a high-born maiden
In a palace tower,
Soothing her love-laden
Soul in secret hour
With music sweet as love, which overflows her bower:

Like a glow-worm golden
In a dell of dew,
Scattering unbeholden
Its aërial hue
Among the flowers and grass which screen it from the view:

Like a rose embower'd
In its own green leaves,
By warm winds deflower'd,
Till the scent it gives
Makes faint with too much sweet these heavy-wingèd thieves:

Sound of vernal showers
On the twinkling grass,
Rain-awaken'd flowers –
All that ever was
Joyous and clear and fresh – thy music doth surpass.

Teach us, sprite or bird,
What sweet thoughts are thine:
I have never heard
Praise of love or wine
That panted forth a flood of rapture so divine.

Chorus hymeneal,
Or triumphal chant,
Match'd with thine would be all
But an empty vaunt –
A thing wherein we feel there is some hidden want.

What objects are the fountains
Of thy happy strain?
What fields, or waves, or mountains?
What shapes of sky or plain?
What love of thine own kind? what ignorance of pain?

With thy clear keen joyance
Languor cannot be:
Shadow of annoyance
Never came near thee:
Thou lovest, but ne'er knew love's sad satiety.

Waking or asleep,
Thou of death must deem
Things more true and deep
Than we mortals dream,
Or how could thy notes flow in such a crystal stream?

We look before and after,
And pine for what is not:
Our sincerest laughter
With some pain is fraught;
Our sweetest songs are those that tell of saddest thought.

Yet, if we could scorn
Hate and pride and fear,
If we were things born
Not to shed a tear,
I know not how thy joy we ever should come near.

Better than all measures
Of delightful sound,
Better than all treasures
That in books are found,
Thy skill to poet were, thou scorner of the ground!

Teach me half the gladness
That thy brain must know;
Such harmonious madness
From my lips would flow,
The world should listen then, as I am listening now.

ENGLISH POET PERCY BYSSHE SHELLEY (1792–1822)

It is one of the first days of Spring, and I sit once more in the Old Garden where I hear no faintest echo of the obscene rumbling of the London streets which are yet so little away. Here the only movement I am conscious of is that of the trees shooting forth their first sprays of bright green, and of the tulips expanding the radiant beauty of their flaming globes, and the only sound I hear is the blackbird's song – the liquid softly gurgling notes that seem to well up spontaneously from an infinite joy, an infinite peace, at the heart of nature and bring a message not from some remote Heaven of the Sky or Future, but the Heaven that is Here, beneath our feet, even beneath the exquisite texture of our own skins, the joy, the peace, at the Heart of the Mystery which is Man. For man alone can hear the Revelation that lies in the blackbird's song.

BRITISH WRITER, SCIENTIST AND REFORMER HAVELOCK ELLIS (1859–1939)

~~~~~~~~~~~~~~~~~~~~~~~~~~~~~~

Be grateful for luck. Pay the thunder no mind –
listen to the birds. And don't hate nobody.

US JAZZ COMPOSER EUBIE BLAKE (1887–1973)

~~~~~~~~~~~~~~~~~~~~~~~~~~~~~~

IN THE GARDEN

Clean bird feeders in late summer

Many birds disappear from our gardens in the second half of the summer, at the end of the breeding season, to take advantage of all the seeds, berries, grains and fruits available around harvest time not just on farmland but also on scrubland and roadside verges. This 'vacation' provides a perfect opportunity to give an extra-thorough scrub-down to feeders and bird tables before the birds start to return in great numbers around the time of the first frosts. This cleansing is vital to help reduce the spread of disease amongst birds.

Let the feeders soak for a few minutes in a solution of 9 parts water to 1 part of a disinfectant, such as bleach or Dettol (or you can buy special bird-feeder solution) and then scrub them with a brush before rinsing them thoroughly and leaving them to dry (a wire-stemmed brush is ideal for tube feeders). It's a good idea to clean feeders as often as possible throughout the year, perhaps rotating them with others, so that there is a constant supply of food. Bird tables and baths should be cleared of debris every day and scrubbed once a week as they are likely to contain droppings which pass on many common avian diseases. You should always wear gloves when washing feeders, tables or water containers. It's also important to move feeders and tables to different positions in the garden, perhaps every two weeks, to prevent the build-up of disease-carrying material on the ground below.

Why Don't Birds Wee?

BIRDS AND THEIR BODIES

Why do birds moult?

Without a full set of good quality feathers a bird will soon die. Birds suffer a lot of wear and tear in their everyday lives and that eventually takes its toll on their plumage. They fly in and out of bushes or reeds, getting snagged by branches, twigs and thorns, they are constantly exposed to the elements and they are riddled with parasites which they often try to pick or rub off. A bird's plumage has to be in good condition in order for it to be able to fly efficiently, which it needs to do to gather its daily quota of food and to avoid being caught by a predator. Furthermore, birds must maintain a very high body temperature and they can't have shabby feathers undermining their insulation. Many male birds also attract a mate by having the best plumage in town, transforming themselves into colourful, immaculately presented creatures at the start of the breeding season. As any peacock will tell you, scruffy birds don't pull. Males aren't going to throw away millions of years of hard evolutionary work with some slack grooming.

The depths to which emperors will sink

It is easy to forget that penguins are birds, since they can't fly and they spend more time in the water than they do on the land. Emperor penguins, in particular, seem to have more in common with the fish they eat than with their feathered cousins. Holding their breath for up to 20 minutes, emperors can dive up to 550 metres (1,800 feet), deeper than any other bird, and deeper than the height of the Empire State Building. Mostly, they stay within 200 metres of the surface to find fish, squid and krill to eat, but if needs must, their extraordinary physiology allows them to plunge to far greater depths in the freezing waters of the Southern Ocean around Antarctica. Emperors, the largest of the penguins with an average height of 1.15m and weight of 32kg, have a highly efficient form of haemoglobin that makes use of every last iota of available oxygen. After a particularly deep dive, they have virtually no oxygen left in their respiratory system or blood but the vital organs still operate long after they would have packed up in any other animal. To help preserve oxygen, the emperors' heart rate can drop to just five or six beats per minute.

Why do the birds we eat have white and dark meat?

The most active muscles of edible birds are full of blood vessels so that they receive a lot of oxygen. These become dark, while the less active, better rested muscles remain white. Turkeys, chickens, quail, pheasants and other gallinaceous birds spend most of their time running on the ground, so their legs and thighs produce the darkest meat. The breast muscles of these birds, which are used for flying, are exercised very rarely, so the meat is white.

Some of my best friends are vultures

The vulture is an ugly bird with terrible table manners that wees on itself and eats dead bodies. It also has a charmless habit of vomiting a foul-smelling gunk over any other animal stupid enough to prey upon it. It is not difficult to see how it has never won a place in our hearts: 'Vulture, Queen of Birds' will never sound right. The vulture is a fascinating creature, however, and it has more human friends than you might have thought, given its etiquette issues. It operates in extreme temperatures. High up in the sky, where the vultures soar and scan the horizon for prey, it is bitterly cold and they have thick plumage to keep themselves warm, but down on the ground, especially in Africa and Asia, the temperature can be overwhelmingly hot. To help them cool down, they have developed a technique, known as urohydrosis, of spraying urine on themselves which then evaporates. (Storks also do this.) The urine also has a sterilizing effect, killing off any germs they may have picked up from the rotten carcasses on which they have fed. In recent years, this unloved bird has attracted a growing band of admirers and supporters in the United States, where the populations of the two species found there, the turkey vulture and the black vulture, have been growing sharply. More cars means more roadkill means more vultures, but more roadkill also means more germs and diseases. The vultures have earned the nickname 'Nature's garbage disposal system' as a tribute to the way they clear up all the carcasses on the nation's roads.

Why do birds lay eggs and not give birth like the rest of us warm-blooded vertebrates?

A bird needs to fly to survive and to fly it needs to be as light as possible for as long as possible. Incredibly, it takes a bird just 24 hours to produce and lay an egg, but this speed is very sensible because it means that the bird is never grounded and can continue to search for food and flee from predators. A bird would barely get airborne if it had evolved to carry its young around inside it. Imagine a heavily pregnant female human trying to sprint 100 metres and then do the high jump. You get the picture. The avian system of laying and then incubating an egg also means that the female can rope the male into a much greater share of the work involved in reproduction: helping with duties around the nest, including taking his turn to sit on the eggs and later tend to the hatchlings.

Why don't vultures have feathers on their head and neck?

Vultures feed by sticking their heads into carcasses, covering head and neck in blood, fat and entrails. So evolution has removed the boring job of cleaning them by getting rid of the feathers altogether.

Grit to the mill

It's easy to see why so many birds are happy to eat seeds and nothing but seeds. Seeds are nature's power food, crammed with goodness and energy to help them transform into young plants with the potential to grow dozens of feet into the air and/or bear pounds and pounds of fruit. But plants guard their offspring every bit as zealously as animals, encasing their seeds in tough outer shells to give them a chance of surviving. In response, birds have acquired powerful beaks and remarkable digestive systems, as well as the skills to prise out the goodness from the seeds and nuts. In the absence of teeth to do the grinding, the stomachs of seed-eating birds such as sparrows and pigeons have evolved into highly effective milling machines, which produce

digestive juices in a first chamber, then churn the seeds with the powerful muscles of the second chamber, in the gizzard. To help the milling process, the birds also eat dozens, even hundreds, of small bits of grit. In larger seed-eaters like chickens, turkeys and, at the extreme end of the scale, the flightless ostrich, the gizzard is bigger and holds more grit because such birds don't have to worry about being too heavy to get airborne.

An ostrich at London Zoo was once found to have swallowed an alarm clock, a roll of film, a handkerchief, a metre-long piece of rope, a cycle valve, a pencil, three gloves, a collar stud, a Belgian franc, four halfpennies and two farthings. Most ostriches in the wild settle for small stones to help them digest not only seeds but also crunchy insects and tougher vegetable matter such as the pods of the acacia tree and aloe plants.

Feathers are what make birds unique

No other creature has them. Others can fly (insects, bats, some squir-rels, some lizards), others lay eggs (reptiles, fishing insects and two weird mammals), and plenty of other creatures are warm-blooded vertebrates. Feathers are the one feature that makes a bird unlike any other living thing.

Do birds get fat?

Fat birds don't make great fliers so most are programmed to stay trim in order to maintain their aviation efficiency. Birds also burn up cal-ories at an incredibly fast rate in their manic, energy-sapping lifestyle. Flying, in particular, is an exhausting business and as birds spend much of their day in the air looking for food they are burning off energy almost as quickly as they're consuming it. The sedentary life is not an option for birds. Whereas many mammals can go weeks without food, most birds will die within a few days. Starvation is the biggest cause of death among birds, even in countries like Britain that are comparatively rich in plants and insects, and in rodents for the birds of prey. There simply isn't enough food to go round. In most bird species, those who live in an area rich in food sources are the lucky minority.

Migratory birds, however, are the exceptions to the rule that birds don't get fat. Swallows, swifts and martins eat insects on the wing as they travel back and forth between southern Africa and Europe, so their weight never changes significantly, but other migratory birds, especially waders, put on huge amounts of fat to sustain them on their long journeys. Fat makes an excellent fuel because it is lighter than carbohydrate and protein and, gram for gram, the bird gets twice as much energy from it. As the time to migrate approaches, birds go into an eating frenzy triggered by an automatic increase in appetite. This gorging process, known as hyperphagia, begins about two to three weeks before the birds take wing for foreign climes, increasing their weight by about 2 per cent per day – though some birds can pile on as much as 10 per cent by the time the sun sets. At the same time, changes in the bird's physiology improve the way they produce and store fat.

Birds that don't migrate usually carry about 3–5 per cent fat; birds flying shorter distances need a 'fat load' of between 10 and 25 per cent; while the longer-distance migrants need anywhere between 40 per cent and, in the case of some warblers, a scales-busting 100 per cent, to give them the energy they need for their epic transcontinental flights. These birds hit their weight limits shortly before setting out over the most challenging geographical features of their journey, such as deserts, mountain ranges, oceans and seas.

Penguins are probably the birds with the most consistently high fat level because, having evolved into aquatic creatures no longer needing to fly, there's no reason for them to be light. On the contrary, given the temperatures they have to withstand, the more fat the better to insulate them and to enable them to survive sometimes prolonged periods without food.

Why don't woodpeckers get headaches or knock themselves out?

When a woodpecker hammers away at a tree trunk to search for insects or to mark out its territory – hundreds of times per minute in some species – the blows from its chisel-like beak crack into the wood at roughly 20mph. In other birds, just one blow of such force would be enough to render them unconscious, but the woodpecker has evolved a highly efficient system for stopping the shock passing straight to its brain. The skull is much thicker than in other birds and its small brain is positioned better to withstand the repeated shocks. The bones connecting the beak to the skull are not as solid and inflexible, and the joints are connected with elastic, highly malleable tissues. Strong neck muscles provide the force for drilling while also absorbing some of the shock. In a neat finish to its physiological design, evolution has endowed the woodpecker with stiff little feathers to shield its nostrils from the flying debris, while its eyes produce a coating of thick membrane that acts like a pair of workman's goggles.

> A bird came down the walk
> He did not know I saw
> He bit an angleworm in halves
> And ate the fellow raw.
> **EMILY DICKINSON**

Why do beaks come in so many different shapes and sizes?

All beaks have evolved to help birds catch their food in the most suitable way possible. Birds of prey have short, sharp, hooked beaks ideal for ripping flesh; finches and sparrows have short, stubby, 'general purpose' beaks for gathering small seeds and insects; the long, needle-like beak of the hummingbird is just the right shape for inserting into narrow flowers, while the long, chisel-like beak of the woodpecker is ideal for drilling wood and chipping away bark. The flamingo has a boomerang-shaped beak which it uses as both a scoop and a sieve while it forages through shallow lakes and lagoons, filtering out all impurities from a mouthful of water and leaving only the micro-organisms. Turnstones creep over rocky shores using their

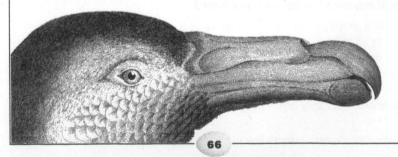

short anvil-shaped bill to hunt food under pebbles. The name of the spoonbill gives away the shape of its beak, which it moves rapidly from side to side while advancing through the shallows, snapping shut on any crustaceans or small fish along the way. As a group, shorebirds have developed the most extraordinary range of beaks so as to avoid competition with one another for the food available in the often narrow or limited feeding areas on coastlines, mudflats and estuaries. A long-billed shorebird and a short-billed species will both eat insect larvae but, as they are working at different depths, they each get what they want without depriving the other. Shorebirds with long beaks often have long legs, enabling them to wade and probe at the same time, and avoid competition with their shorter-billed chums back at the water's edge.

A wonderful bird is the pelican,
His bill can hold more than his belican,
He can take in his beak,
Food enough for a week,
But I'm damned if I see how the helican.
**US POET AND HUMORIST DIXON LANIER MERRIT
(1879–1954)**

The Australian pelican has the longest beak of all birds, measuring up to 47cm, but the longest beak in relation to body length is that of the sword-billed hummingbird of South America. At 5cm, the beak is longer than the body and the bird has to groom itself with its feet.

Why does the puffin have such a charming beak?

The puffin's colourful, triangular beak has caught the imagination of people for centuries; if evolution were ever to replace it with something more drab and functional it's unlikely the bird would get a second glance, let alone have a famous publishing imprint named after it. Resembling a cross between a parrot and a penguin, the puffin is sometimes affectionately referred to as 'the clown of the sea', but the large red, yellow and blue beak, protruding from between its doleful eyes, has not been stuck at the top of its plump black and white body just so that humans can sit around sighing with pleasure at the sight of it. It is there for a serious purpose. Just as other birds sport more colourful plumage to attract a mate, so the puffin grows a colourful beak. In most birds it is the males alone who turn on the colour in the breeding season, but with the puffins it is both sexes. The orange of the birds' feet also becomes brighter in the breeding season, while the beak grows a little bit longer each year. The size and colour of the beaks are key factors by which the birds assess the fitness of potential partners.

The beaks are also highly efficient fishing tools, featuring backward-pointing spikes that enable them to gather dozens of small fish in one trip. Some seabirds swallow their catch and then regurgitate it for their chicks, but the puffin stacks the fish crosswise in its mouth, allowing it to save energy by taking one long foraging trip.

Once the breeding season is over, the colourful outer cases of the beak fall away to reveal an altogether duller object.

Where do birds sleep?

While owls, nightjars and other nocturnal birds head out into the gloom for a late evening meal, the rest of the bird world retires to sleep after another long, exhausting day foraging for food and dodging the cat. Most birds head to a roosting site where they will be safe from predators and protected from the elements. The body temperature of most species will drop by about a fifth to conserve energy and many species huddle together at night, especially in winter, to keep warm. Birds effectively spend the night in a state of hypothermia. Evolution having endowed them with the ability to maintain their balance and grip while they snooze, most songbirds will spend the night perched on a branch with their heads turned round and their beaks buried in their plumage. The way birds sleep varies between species and there is still much scientists don't know about avian sleep patterns. Many sleep in very short bursts to keep alert for predators while others have developed the ability to sleep with one eye open. Swifts and swallows sleep on the wing for a few seconds at a time high up in the sky, while the wandering albatross, a bird that flies all the way round the lower half of the world in a single journey in search of food, sleeps as it soars above the icebergs below. Ducks and other aquatic birds will sleep on land but many choose to spend the night on the water to avoid predators. Ducks sleep in a line with two on the ends keeping an eye open for intruders.

from **The Owl against Robin**
Frowning, the owl in the oak complained him
Sore, that the song of the robin restrained him
Wrongly of slumber, rudely of rest.
'From the north, from the east, from the south and the west,
Woodland, wheat-field, corn-field, clover,
Over and over and over and over,
Five o'clock, ten o'clock, twelve, or seven,
Nothing but robin-songs heard under heaven:
How can we sleep?'

US POET SIDNEY LANIER (1842–81)

Why is bird poo white?

In a roundabout way, like so many answers to questions about birds, it's all to do with flying. The science of this subject doesn't yield its explanation easily, but bear with me – imagine how people around the table will gasp when you clear your throat and announce: 'I know why bird plop is white . . .'

With the exception of vultures and some storks, birds don't urinate because, as creatures that live and die by their ability to fly efficiently, they cannot afford to be weighed down by excess moisture. If a bird did urinate, it would have to consume such massive quantities of water it would spend most of its day drinking. But birds must still expel the potentially fatal toxins, including ammonia, which form when their food is broken down in the digestive system and its nitrogen content makes new compounds. Mammals get rid of nitrogen via their urine by making a less toxic yellow compound called urea, which needs a lot of water to flush it through. Hence urine is mainly water. On average mammals lose 30 times more water in expelling nitrogen waste than birds do. Birds get rid of their nitrogen by transforming it into a toxic compound called uric acid, made of tiny *white* crystals, which cannot be urinated away because it is not water-soluble like urea. The bird's incredibly efficient digestive system absorbs almost every last drop of water that passes through the body, allowing it to go comparatively long periods without a drink as well as survive in some of the world's most arid and unforgiving climates.

Why don't ducks mind getting wet?

Water really does just slide off a duck's back, as it does with most aquatic birds like swans, grebes and coots – and to a slightly lesser extent with nearly all birds. The plumage of a duck works in the same way as an oiled waterproof coat. Using its beak, the duck takes the waxy substance from a preening gland beneath its tail and wipes it over its body. Thousands of downy feathers under the plumage help to trap the air and preserve body temperature in cold water. Sometimes this can make a bird that dives for its food too buoyant, so it will dive down to expel the trapped air.

Cormorants and shags are the only water-based birds that don't have waterproof plumage. It is thought that this may help them dive more quickly to catch their prey since their sodden feathers do not retain air bubbles. After fishing, cormorants go ashore and hold out their wings to dry in the sun.

Why don't birds have penises?

There are a number of sensible reasons why evolution has shunned the penis option for most birds. Evolution has done everything in its gift to adapt birds for efficient flight. A bird must fly light so a penis – complete with compulsory external testicles – would be unwelcome excess baggage for nature's aviators. (Male birds do have gonads, buried deep inside the body, but they are tiny outside the breeding season.) Evolution has also worked out that it would be a poorly designed bird indeed that carried vulnerable dangly bits on its underside as it swooped in and out of bushes so many hundreds of times a day. Nor would it be a great idea for birds to mate by coupling together for more than a few seconds, what with so many sharp-clawed predators about. Birds need to escape in an instant and that's not so easy if they're lying on the lawn, locked in heavenly transport, making the bird with two backs. So both males and females have ended up with the cloaca and copulation lasts no longer than the shake of a tail.

Plain tasteless

Birds have a very poor sense of taste. It varies slightly from species to species but on average they have about 50 taste buds, compared to 9,000 in humans. Without teeth, birds swallow their food whole, leaving it to their powerful stomachs to break down the food.

A handful of birds including ducks, geese, ostriches and flamingos do have penises. The duck has one because it mates on water and the female is half-submerged during copulation. If it mated like other birds, with male and female touching cloacas, the droplet containing the sperm would be washed away, so a drake needs a penis to make sure the sperm is delivered safely. The male Argentine lake duck has the longest penis of all vertebrates, measuring a whopping 42.5cm, roughly the same length as the bird itself. (Other male ducks have to take consolation from the fact that the lake duck has the brains and personality of a dead fish, a really irritating quack and unattractive plumage.) In all ducks, the penis, like the female's vagina, is shaped like a corkscrew. The unusual shape of the penis allows the duck to keep it wound up inside until he needs it.

Tongue-tied woodpeckers

At 10cm, the tongue of the woodpecker is four times longer than its beak and has to be curled round inside beneath the skin when it's not being used. The sticky tongue, which has sharp barbs on the end, is used for extracting the ants from deep in their nest. Ants are a staple part of the green woodpecker's diet: it will eat as many as 2,000 in a day and travel many miles to find them.

Sac de merde

Many birds, especially the smaller, defenceless ones, hide their nests to avoid their young being taken by predators and they go to great lengths to make sure they don't leave a trail of evidence to alert attackers to their whereabouts. Dumping excreta all over surrounding branches and leaves would be an obvious giveaway and so many chicks have developed the neat trick of shitting into a little internal sac. The parent pecks the chick on the bum and out comes a little white bag of faeces which the parent proceeds to swallow. When the chick grows older and its faeces are less digestible, the parents carry the shit-sac from the nest and dump it at a safe distance. Just as humans do with nappies.

This season's fashion

When they moult, most birds lose a few feathers at a time, replacing the whole plumage over the course of one or two months, so as not to undermine their flying efficiency or insulation. For the majority of birds the moult comes at the end of the breeding season when their feathers are in a tattered state after months of hectic activity. Moulting also uses up a lot of energy so late summer and early autumn is the best time of year because it is the least stressful and exhausting. The chicks have fledged and are out there fending for themselves, there is plenty of food around, it's not too cold and there is still thick foliage in which the more vulnerable birds can spend much of the day hidden from predators.

Most adult birds moult only once a year, but the current year's hatch will often renew their feathers three times before donning their adult plumage the spring after they were born. Though a few wait till afterwards, the majority of migratory birds moult shortly before they set off so that their feathers are in top aerodynamic condition for the long journey ahead. Some species moult twice a year, adopting a more colourful appearance in the breeding season. Birds of prey, which need to stay airborne to survive by hunting, moult in a constant process throughout the year.

Ducks do it naked

Unlike most other birds, ducks, geese and swans lose all their flight feathers at once, rendering them flightless for a period. They hide in reeds and rushes until new feathers grow, often congregating in a remote place in large numbers for safety reasons. If attacked by a predator their chances of survival are greater in a group than if they were alone. The male duck sheds the brightly coloured plumage it wore for courting its partner, donning dull brown feathers, known as 'eclipse' plumage, that make it virtually indistinguishable from the female for a few months.

Why are flamingos pink?

The stunning pink plumage of the flamingo is caused by the beta-carotene in its diet of shrimps and blue-green algae, which are both rich in the pigment. When deprived of these food sources in zoos, the flamingo turns white unless it is fed other foods rich in beta-carotene such as carrots, beetroots and sweet red peppers. (Salmon is pink because its diet includes crustaceans that contain the carotene.) You, too, can turn flamingo pink if you wish – if you're prepared to eat beetroot for breakfast, lunch and dinner for a few weeks!

Bird body facts

- The four toes of passerines, or songbirds, are designed and arranged for perching, with three pointing forward and one pointing back.

- No bird has teeth. Evolution has disposed of them to lighten the load and improve flying efficiency.

- All birds have tongues.

- Birds don't sweat. To lose heat, they pant and head for shade.

- As a general rule, the bigger the bird, the less it eats. Birds of prey eat a quarter of their weight every day, songbirds about half, while tiny hummingbirds consume twice their body mass in energy-boosting nectar.

Necking drinks

Most birds can't suck so they drink by taking a beak of water and then tipping back their heads. Only a handful of birds, including pigeons and doves, are able to use their tongues to consume water without having to tilt their necks.

A sight better

Sight is a bird's best sense. Its hearing is good as well – exceptional in most nocturnal species – but a bird lives or dies by the quality of its vision. A human being can lead a perfectly satisfactory life with poor eyesight, but a bird in need of spectacles would perish very quickly. A bird's visual abilities are without equal in the animal kingdom, enabling it to carry out a wide range of crucial functions. Many birds fly at great speed through dense foliage and in dim light, and most have to be on the constant lookout for predators. A bird needs to locate food quickly and accurately. In the never-ending desperate quest for the energy it needs to maintain its highly demanding metabolism, it cannot afford to waste time flitting about the shrubbery sampling different insects and plants, mistaking grit for seed or, worse still, poisoning itself by wrongly identifying a specimen. Nor can it risk making itself vulnerable to predator attack by alighting on the ground or a branch for more than a few seconds. A female also needs to be able to assess the fitness of a potential partner by a close inspection of minute, telltale physical characteristics such as the colour quality of the suitor's plumage. It's unhelpful, though, to make generalizations about avian vision because there are wide variations between orders of birds. Comparisons with other creatures are not that useful either because the way in which birds see is different.

Birds who have what their names suggest

Redwing
Crossbill
Blackcap
Spoonbill
Goldeneye
Goldcrest
Whitethroat
Razorbill
Pintail

Eyes like tea saucers

If our eyes were in the same proportion to our heads as those of birds, we'd all be looking at the world through facial features the size of tea saucers and tennis balls. Apart from making it extremely difficult for anyone to take anyone else remotely seriously ever again, it would also mean that our brains would have to shrink in order to accommodate our massive eyeballs. Birds have the largest eyes relative to body size of all terrestrial vertebrates and their brains are amongst the smallest. The skull of a mammal is filled up mainly with brain, but in birds it is the eye that takes up most room. Some hawks and owls have eyes as large as human eyes, even though in overall body size they are between 120 and 150 times smaller. At 5cm in diameter, the eye of the ostrich is the largest of any land animal. In some owls, the eyes make up over 30 per cent of the weight of the head whereas in humans it is only about 1 per cent – even though humans have exceptionally efficient sight as well.

It's all a bit of a blur for the scientists

Unable to sit birds down in front of an optician's letter chart and ask them to squawk what they see, scientists still have a great deal they don't know about the quality of avian vision. It is clear, though, even to the layman, that there is a great deal of discrepancy between the species. A domesticated chicken, one of the easier birds to test, has poor eyesight for the simple reason that there is no evolutionary pressure for it to see well. Unlike most birds, the chicken doesn't fly in and out of dense foliage as songbirds do, and it doesn't have to look very hard for its food as almost all wild birds do. More often than not, its food is right under its beak, placed there by a human being with dark plans to roast it or scramble its eggs.

Songbirds and birds of prey are thought to be able to focus on objects two or three times further away than humans can, with no more than a quick glance. In the retina of an animal eye there are thousands of receptor cells, and the more cells it has the sharper the images it sees. The human eye has about 200,000 cones per square

millimetre, while the songbirds in your garden have roughly double that. Birds of prey, hovering and soaring to spot small mammals often hundreds of feet below, have four to six times as many as humans. The speed with which birds process information from visual sources may also be a factor. It is thought that many orders and species are able to understand what they are looking at with the merest glance whereas it may take humans and other mammals much longer.

Night goggles

A barn owl can spot prey in light so poor that were humans endowed with the equivalent ability we would be able to pick out an object by the light of a match over a mile away.

Why do some birds have eyes on the side of their heads and others on the front?

Most birds have eyes on the side rather than the front of their heads because it gives them better panoramic vision to help spot predators and food sources. When you see a thrush hopping about on the lawn with its head tilted to one side, it is looking for worms and not, as often thought, listening out for them.

The woodcock has the best all-round vision: its eyes are positioned so far back in its head that it has a 360-degree view of its world without having to move its head.

But birds with good field of vision are unable to judge distance and perspective as well as creatures with binocular vision. Birds of prey, such as hawks, owls and eagles, are exceptions in the bird world in having eyes on the front of their heads, giving them the binocular or stereoscopic vision they need to see depth. A bird of prey needs to judge distance to exact measurements when diving and stooping at great speed to take its victim. To compensate for their smaller field of vision, birds of prey have developed the ability to rotate their heads all the way round.

Do birds see in colour?

Birds' colour vision is far more developed and sophisticated than ours. It enables them to spot prey at a distance and distinguish between good and bad sources of food, and allows females to make out minute differences in the quality of plumage when deciding which partner to take at the start of the breeding season. Like a woman being able to tell the colour of a man's eyes or the cut of his suit from 100 paces, a female bird quickly works out the potential fitness of the suitor trying to impress her with his appearance. Scruffy, dull characters need not apply. Many birds – notably hummingbirds – have the ability to see ultraviolet light (shared with nectar-hunting insects), which helps them spy out their food sources of flowers and fruit. Owls, and other nocturnal birds, are exceptions to the general rule because good colour vision would reduce the sensitivity of their sight in dim light.

No need to shout, I'm an owl

As most owls operate in the twilight hours of dawn and dusk – only a few species are strictly nocturnal – evolution has equipped them with a wide range of ingenious physical gifts and gadgets including superb camouflage, keen eyesight and a feather structure that allows them to swoop silently upon their prey. Above all, it is the astonishingly efficient if bizarre hearing system of the owl that sets it apart

from its feathered colleagues; an owl can locate its prey by detecting the smallest rustle in the undergrowth. It has one ear set very marginally higher than the other and this asymmetry gives it the aural equivalent of binocular vision. The minuscule time difference between the sound being perceived in one ear and in the other provides a cross reference from which the owl can work out the exact location of its source.

The region of the brain which controls hearing is three to five times more developed in the owl than in most other birds and although its range of audible sounds is roughly the same as for humans its hearing is much more acute at certain frequencies.

The owl may be dozens of yards away sitting on a branch or gliding through the air but once it picks up the merest tremor of sound it will pinpoint its prey to within millimetres. If the animal moves, the owl's brain, moving faster than the most advanced GPS system, is able to make virtually instant recalculations as it swoops in for the kill. The owl has memorized every square inch of its terrain. Once the owl's hearing has locked on, the prey has no chance of survival even if it is buried under two feet of heavily impacted snow or thick brush.

The strictly nocturnal species, such as the barn owl, have the additional advantage of a round, hollowed-out face which operates like a radar dish, collecting and channelling sounds into the ear openings. An owl's ears are positioned at the sides of its head, covered by the feathers of the facial disc. The pointy tufts sported by some species, such as the long-eared owl, are not ears at all but display feathers.

Taking the sting out of it

Bee-eaters need several hundred bees every day to feed their young and give themselves the extra energy required for the frenetic hunting in the breeding season. They take the sting out of bees by rubbing or whacking them to death on their perch.

Eiderdown ... and almost out

Down feathers, the fluffy under-layer closest to the skin of ducks, geese and other aquatic birds, are amongst nature's best insulating materials. The warmest down comes from the eider duck, the UK's heaviest duck and the fastest through the air. It is a sea duck that spends much of its year inside the Arctic Circle and has developed its remarkable down in order to survive in freezing conditions. Eider down has been so sought after by man that by the end of the nineteenth century the bird was almost extinct. Its numbers have recovered but they are threatened once again – this time because the eider duck's dependence on coastal molluscs has brought it into conflict with mussel farmers.

Useless nostrils

Sight and hearing are the senses that a bird relies on for its survival. Birds have the equipment to smell, but the ability has been developed only in a tiny handful of the world's 10,000 species, most notably the kiwi. Many seabirds, too, including the shearwater, the fulmar and the storm-petrel, Britain's smallest breeding seabird, have evolved with a very strong sense of smell to help them detect food sources at sea.

Most birds have two external, unobtrusive nostrils, or *nares*, located on the upper mandible of their beaks, which they use for breathing. Some diving species such as gannets, shags and cormorants don't have nostrils and breathe through the beak instead. Anyone who has jumped awkwardly into a swimming pool and felt a blast of water up their nose will understand why evolution has sealed up the nostrils of these birds.

Why don't penguins freeze to death when they moult?

Unlike most birds, that moult slowly, generally over a period of six to eight weeks, the penguin renews its feathers as quickly as possible. Most penguins take no more than two or three weeks to produce a fresh warm coat of feathers in a process known as a 'catastrophic moult'. They adopt this approach because even more than other birds they need to be waterproof and well insulated from the cold to maintain their aquatic lifestyle. A couple of weeks before the moult they start gorging food to put on as much weight as possible, almost doubling their body mass. During the moult they stay out of the water and live off their fat whilst their new feathers push out the old ones. The penguins huddle together to keep warm, rotating positions to make sure each does its turn on the freezing, wind-battered fringes of the group before returning to the relative heat of the centre, which is roughly 10°C warmer than the edges.

Quite a stink

The long-running debate as to whether vultures locate carrion by sight or smell included a famous transatlantic stink in the early nineteenth century between the American artist and ornithologist John James Audubon and Charles 'Squire' Waterton, an eccentric British naturalist and explorer who used to enjoy imitating a dog and biting the legs of his guests under the dinner table. The argument still hasn't been completely settled but what the experts know for sure is that the turkey vulture, a species found in the Americas, definitely forages for carrion by smell. All the others, including the African and Asian species, almost certainly use their sight, even if some can smell a little. From experiments carried out in the

Birds are more colourful in the gentler light of early morning and late afternoon because the harsh glare of the midday sun makes their plumage appear paler.

1960s, we now know that the turkey vulture picks up the smell of mercaptan, a gas produced by decaying flesh, and will be first on the scene as a result. Spotting its turkey vulture cousin tearing at the flesh, the larger black vulture will arrive and bully its way to the carcass, sticking its neck through the mouth and anus of the carcass to pull out its entrails. (Don't, whatever you do, try this at home. You'll never get the stains off your shirt collar.) The king vulture, yet bigger and more powerful, is next to reach the feast, and then it is the black vultures who must defer and step aside. And if there's a condor, one of the world's largest birds, in the vicinity, everyone else has to make way until the carcass has been torn wide open and the condor has eaten its fill.

Why does the toucan have such an enormous beak?

The giant, bright orange beak of the toucan, measuring more than half the length of the body in some cases, is what makes the bird one of the most instantly recognizable of the world's 10,000 species. But why it has such an extraordinary beak is a mystery the ornithologists have yet to crack. No theory holds water. The beak can't be a weapon because, in spite of its size and solid appearance, it is in fact incredibly lightweight, a honeycomb structure made from a fibrous protein called keratin, from which birds' feathers – and our fingernails – are also made. More feather duster than knuckle duster if it came to a fight. Its lightness explains how a toucan can apparently defy gravity

when perched on a branch. The casual onlooker would think it only a matter of time before the weight of its huge orange mandibles sent the bird crashing to the ground or swinging upside down like a big bat, but the gargantuan beak actually makes up less than one twentieth of the toucan's entire body mass.

The beak may come in handy for plucking fruits on branches far away from those strong enough to support the bird's weight, but the experts are not convinced that this is the one and only reason that evolution would go to such lengths to produce, well, such a length. Nor does the beak appear to have been adapted for a particular style of eating or hunting. Toucans are not specialist feeders. They consume a lot of fruit and berries, but most species will also eat seeds, insects and even snakes, frogs, small mammals and the eggs of other birds. You don't need a beak the size of Cuba to eat any of the above, as many other bird species demonstrate. Nor do scientists believe that the beaks play a part in attracting a mate during the breeding season.

Although the birds will use their beaks to toss each other fruit, especially when they're feeling flirtatious and playful in the breeding season, evolution will not have spent millions of years developing this frankly ridiculous and mildly unsettling feature just so the birds can have a good old food fight. But at a stage in our civilization when scientists appear to know virtually everything there is to know about the natural world in which we live, isn't it wonderful that they still can't solve the mystery of the toucan's beak?

A Complex Relationship

BIRDS AND MAN

George V of England had a pink-grey pet parrot called Charlotte which he kept in his study at Sandringham and carried around with him, perched on his fingers or shoulder. Queen Mary was not amused by his habit of letting Charlotte wander across the breakfast table, unloading droppings amongst the marmalade pots and devilled kidneys. When the King took to his study to examine the latest batch of state documents, Charlotte sat on his shoulder, squawking loudly: 'Well, what about it?'

I realized that if I had to choose, I would rather have birds than airplanes.

US AVIATOR CHARLES LINDBERGH (1902–74)

⟨ Among those I know of are a Prime Minister, a President, three Secretaries of State, a charwoman, two policemen, two Kings, two Royal Dukes, one Prince, one Princess, a Communist, seven Labour, one Liberal, six Conservative Members of Parliament, several farm-labourers earning ninety shillings a week, a rich man who earns two or three times more than that every hour of the day, at least forty-six schoolmasters, an engine-driver, a postman, and an upholsterer. ⟩

BRITISH ORNITHOLOGIST, NATURALIST, BROADCASTER AND AUTHOR JAMES FISHER (1912–70), WRITING ABOUT THE BIRD LOVERS HE KNEW IN *WATCHING BIRDS*

Why do some people hate cormorants?

If ever you are in any doubt about the evolutionary link between birds and dinosaurs, then take a look at the cormorant. Its long neck, sinister beady eyes and jet black plumage give it an arrestingly pre-historic appearance, more a reptile with feathers and wings than a

God loved the birds and invented trees. Man loved the birds and invented cages.

FRENCH PLAYWRIGHT JACQUES DEVAL (1890–1972), *AFIN DE VIVRE BEL ET BIEN*

bird. Strangely for an aquatic bird, along with its close relative the shag, it has no oil-producing preening gland to water-proof its coat, which you'd think was some-thing of a design fault given that the cormorant spends half its day diving underwater in search of fish. The reason is that, for a diver, buoy-ancy is no advantage; wet plumage helps it descend faster underwater to catch its prey. Consequently, the cormorant spends much of the rest of the day sitting on a rock, holding its wings out to dry in the wind in a pose which only adds to its dinosaur, pterodactyl image. But it's not its slightly creepy silhouette so much as its invasion of Britain's inland waterways that upsets people, most especially our anglers who've been getting their wading pants in a terrible twist over the birds. To them the cormorants are 'the black plague'.

There are only about 10,000 breeding pairs of cormorants in Britain, spread mainly around the coastline, but in winter a further 25,000 arrive and, taking the cue from their freshwater cousins on the continent, they've started to head inland to fish in our rivers, lakes, fisheries and reservoirs, much to the chagrin of our friends in the rubber chest waders. Cormorants are highly efficient at catching fish – so good that the Chinese and Japanese have even trained them to do it for them – and anglers believe that they are exhausting precious stocks, including the young fish. The truth, however, is that there is no hard evidence that cormorants are actually causing more than minor damage. Fish have far more serious pressures, what with pollution, disease, degradation of their habitat – anglers! – and weird, changing weather patterns undermining their own food sources. The

arrival of a few cormorants is the least of a fish's worries. Could it be that anglers returning home bemoaning the 'one that got away' have now found the perfect excuse for their empty-handedness? 'Bloody cormorants!'

The 6th Lord Walsingham (1843–1919) holds the unofficial record for the most varied bag in a day's shooting. In January 1889, he shot 65 coot, 39 pheasant, 23 mallard, 16 rabbit, nine hare, seven teal, six gadwall, six partridge, four pochard duck, three snipe, three swan, two moorhen, two heron, an otter, a woodcock, a wood pigeon, a goldeneye, a rat and, just to prove that not even the fish were safe, a pike he saw in shallow water. Walsingham also holds the individual single-day shooting record for killing 1,070 grouse at Yorkshire's Blubberhouse Moor on 30 August 1888.

Notable letters to *The Times* about birds

From Spike Hughes, 15 June 1962
Sir, All thrushes (not only those in the neck of the Glynde-bourne woods) sooner or later sing the tune of the first subject of Mozart's G minor Symphony (K.550) – and, what's more, phrase it a sight better than most conductors. The tempo is always dead right and there is no suggestion of unauthorized accent on the ninth note of the phrase.

From T. L. Ward, 1 June 1956
Sir, The parliamentary Secretary to the Ministry of Agriculture stated in Parliament recently that the amount of oats issued to racehorses in April was 556 tons, which was considered a comparatively small quantity of grain to divert from human consumption. He did not say, however, that it would have been an adequate grain ration for 300,000 hens which, in April, would have laid at least 6,000,000 eggs.

From the Chancellor of the Exchequer, 24 January 1933
Sir, It may be of interest to record that, in walking through St.
James's Park today, I noticed a grey wagtail running about on
the now temporarily dry bed of the lake, near the dam below the
bridge, and occasionally picking small insects out of the cracks
in the dam.

Probably the occurrence of this in the heart of London has
been recorded before, but I have not myself previously noted it
in the park.

I am your obedient servant,
Neville Chamberlain
PS For the purpose of removing doubts, as we say in the House
of Commons, I should perhaps add that I mean a grey wagtail
and not a pied.

*From Lord Knutsford, 12 August 1914 (a week after Britain
declared war on Germany)*
Sir, In the next few weeks many thousand grouse will be shot. I
suggest that they should be eaten instead of butcher's meat and
not in addition to it. I suggest that it might be well to send large
quantities into cold storage to be used when needed. The same
applies to pheasants and partridges in due course, and to ground
game, and the hospitals would be very grateful for stags.

Why are parrots happy to sit in a cage when most other birds would go mad and die?

Parrots and other pet birds have been bred in captivity and they know no other life. Most wild birds would die in a small cage and the ones that spend almost their entire lives on the wing, like swallows, would die very quickly. Birds would survive in a large outdoor cage that replicates their wild habitat. You don't see many of these in people's gardens, however, for the simple reason that it is illegal to take birds or their eggs from the wild.

Gross domestic product

The economy of the tiny Pacific island of Nauru, a former British colony, was for the entire twentieth century based on the export of ancient bird droppings, making its inhabitants amongst the richest in the world. Three quarters of the island was mined for the rock phosphate made from guano, and its extraction has left hundreds of cone-shaped limestone outcrops that give the landscape a haunting, outer-space appearance. Now that its once fertile land is exhausted of its rich deposits Nauru has become virtually uninhabitable, leaving the remaining islanders in a state of poverty.

I have been guilty of a great mistake. I have wasted my life with mineralogy which has led to nothing . . . Had I devoted myself to birds, their life and plumage, I might have produced something worth doing.

ENGLISH AUTHOR, ARTIST AND CRITIC JOHN RUSKIN (1819–1900)

❝ Anytime you hear a man called "loony" just remember that's a great compliment to the man and a great disrespect to the loon. A loon doesn't wage war, his government is perfect being non-existent. He is the world's best fisherman and completely in control of his senses, thank you. ❞

JEROME LAWRENCE AND ROBERT E. LEE, *THE NIGHT THOREAU SPENT IN JAIL*

Bird omens and superstitions

- A bird in the house is a presage of death or dire ill fortune.

- Two blackbirds together is a good omen. You will be blessed with good luck for a whole year if a blackbird nests in your house.

- The number of notes a cuckoo sings tells the listener how many years he or she has left to live.

- When a swallow stays close to its nest, bad weather is on the way.

- Your house will be protected from lightning if swallows nest under its eaves.

- Ill fortune befalls anyone who harms a wren or its nest.

- The blind will eventually regain their sight if they feed ravens.

- A dove is thought to bring good luck to a marriage. Doves are associated with peace and love as they often mate for life and both partners care for the upbringing of their young.

- The dove is the only bird whose form the devil can't assume.

- It was once thought that gulls and albatrosses carried the souls of dead sailors.

- Many people used to believe that the magpie was the devil in disguise. To dispel the ill fortune he would bring, on encountering the first magpie of the day, you were meant to tilt your hat, cross your fingers and say 'Good morning, Mr Magpie'.

- You are doomed if an owl calls your name, which is damned bad luck if you happen to be called Too-wit-too-woo, or Hoot.

Why do some people start cursing and waving sticks around at the sight of a flock of geese coming in to land?

Canada geese can destroy a lawn or a stretch of park in a couple of hours. Each bird is able to strip out over 100 blades of grass a minute, and will continue to do so, even into the night if there is a bright moon and a clear sky, until a) it gets too dark, b) there is no grass left or c) an angry person with a stick catches up with them. They need to eat material that is readily available and easy to digest, and they need to eat it fast. While they are busy reducing the lawn to an expanse of mud, they add insult to injury by shitting almost as quickly as they eat. Geese have a very basic approach to food and digestion: get it down quick, shit it out quick, then crack on to the next lawn.

The Gettysburg Vultures

Every year hundreds of black vultures and turkey vultures congregate in the Pennsylvania skies above the site of the Battle of Gettysburg. They first appeared on 1 July 1863, the first of three days of intense fighting between Union and Confederate armies in the American Civil War. Each side suffered roughly 20,000 casualties, among the highest of the four-year conflict, and the battlefield was also littered with the bodies of tens of thousands of dead horses, a feast of carrion for the vultures. There was so much food to be had that the birds are said to have stayed the winter and scavenged on the frozen carcasses. Every twelve months since then, for almost 150 years, they have been returning to the same spot. It is a chilling, haunting reminder of one of America's bloodiest days.

Forget Viagra, eat a sparrow

There have been a host of theories put forward to explain the mystery of why the sparrow has been disappearing from our city centres, but perhaps the most outlandish is the one that claims the little birds have all been captured and cooked by sex maniacs who believe that the meat is an aphrodisiac. The sparrow has been associated with lust from Classical times and in the seventeenth century Nicholas Culpeper, a highly influential physician and botanist, wrote without so much as a twitch of irony: 'This is an undeniable aphorism that whatsoever a creature is addicted unto, they move or incite the man or the woman, that eats them, to the like: and therefore partridges, quails, sparrows etc. being extremely addicted to venery, they work the same effect in those men and women that eat them . . . the brain of sparrows when eaten provokes the lust exceedingly.'

Do geese mind being force-fed to make foie gras?

It depends on who you talk to. Put this question to a French restaurant owner or one of the 30,000 people working in France's foie gras industry and you'll probably receive one of the following answers, allowing for some losses in translation:

    a)   Non! Ça ne pose pas de problèmes aux oiseaux.
    b)   Oui, un petit peu but who cares? It's bloody delicious.
    c)   Why don't you bog off and go and see the chicken farmer next door if you want to see real bird cruelty?
    d)   Pardon, je ne comprends pas. Au revoir, Monsieur Rosbif.

Foie gras, French for 'fat liver', is a highly prized and expensive delicacy made from the enlarged liver of a duck or goose. Opponents of its production contend that the force-feeding of large quantities of grain, a process known as *gavage*, causes severe distress to the birds. For the animal rights activist, *gavage* is as cruel as veal production and the fur trade. A foie gras duck or goose is bred specially for the purpose and kept in a small cage so that it can't turn round. When the bird is about two months old, it is force-fed several pounds of fat-soaked cornmeal two or three times a day through a long metal tube inserted deep into its throat. When the liver has expanded many times beyond its natural size, the bird is slaughtered. (Being migratory birds, ducks and geese have a great capacity for putting on weight. In the wild they pile on the pounds to provide them with the energy reserves they need to fly thousands of miles.) The producers say that as ducks and geese don't have a gag reflex and swallow their food whole, *gavage* doesn't bother them. Animal rights activists claim that the birds are not so relaxed about their eccentric feeding arrangements, producing reports of oesophageal wounds, ruptured livers, general ill-health, painful deaths and so forth, to justify their protests.

Foie gras producers counter that even if the claims were true, their opponents would do the cause of animal welfare far more good if they turned their attention to the world's poultry industry, which is responsible for hundreds of millions of animal deaths each year and an immeasurable amount of cruelty to the chickens living in barbaric factory farms. Besides, they say, what business is it of a government or a lobby group to tell people what they should or should not eat?

The football game Subbuteo, a common sight on Britain's carpets in the pre-electronic entertainment age, is called after the proper name of the hobby falcon, *Falco subbuteo*, meaning 'smaller than a buzzard'. The hobby was the favourite bird of the game's designer Peter Adolph.

Bird Watcher

In Wall Street once a potent power,
And now a multi-millionaire
Alone within a shady bower
In clothes his valet would not wear,
He watches bird wings bright the air.

The man who mighty mergers planned,
And oil and coal kinglike controlled,
With field-glasses in failing hand
Spies downy nestlings five days old,
With joy he could not buy for gold.

Aye, even childlike is his glee;
But how he crisps with hate and dread
And shakes a clawlike fist to see
A kestrel hover overhead:
Though he would never shoot it dead.

Although his cook afar doth forage
For food to woo his appetite,
The old man lives on milk and porridge
And now it is his last delight
At eve if one lone linnet lingers
To pick crushed almonds from his fingers.

BRITISH POET ROBERT SERVICE (1874–1958)

Chairman Mao's Great Sparrow Campaign

Sparrows, en masse, can be a nuisance to farmers, munching their way through fields of ripening grain and breaking the stalks when they perch on them. They tend to operate from the safety of a boundary hedge, which is why you may have seen a 3-metre-wide band round the edge of a crop field that has been stripped bare. In 1958 China's Chairman Mao Zedong, leader of the Communist Revolution, who had figured out that each bird eats 5kg of grain every year, tried to exterminate all his country's sparrows in what was called

the Great Sparrow Campaign. This was part of his Four Pests Campaign, an ambitious – some would say utterly insane – plan to rid China of all rats, mosquitoes, flies and sparrows. For the sparrow project, the army roamed the countryside firing shots into the air, while peasants were ordered to leave their homes and bang some pots and pans in a bid to kill the birds by exhausting them. Millions of birds died and thousands of nests were destroyed, but when the harvest yield then went down still further, people realized that the sparrows were needed to keep down the insects eating the crops. Sparrow numbers soon recovered. One–nil to nature.

English poet and painter William Blake on birds:

A robin redbreast in a cage
Puts all heaven in a rage.

He who shall hurt the little wren
Shall never be belov'd by men.

When thou seest an eagle, thou seest a portion of genius;
lift up thy head!

The Owl and the Nightingale

Florence Nightingale saved a baby owl from some boys who were tormenting it at the Parthenon in Athens where she had stopped off on her return from Egypt in 1850. The 'Lady with the Lamp' christened the owl Athena, smuggled it aboard her ship and took it back to England where it became something of an attraction in the Nightingale household, perching on Florence's fingers to feed and happily sitting in her pocket as she went about her daily business. When Nightingale came back from the Crimea in 1856, after tending to the injured soldiers of the British Army, her family rushed to greet her in London, leaving Athena in the attic of the family home. When the gathering returned, they hurried upstairs to see Athena, only to find her lying on her back, claws in the air, dead as a dodo. Florence, so stoical in her military field hospitals, burst into tears on the spot. The bird was stuffed and can be seen today in the Florence Nightingale Museum at St Thomas's Hospital in London.

~~~~~

She was not quite what you would call refined. She was not quite what you would call unrefined. She was the kind of person that keeps a parrot.

US AUTHOR MARK TWAIN
(1835–1910)

~~~~~

~~~~~~~~~~~~~~~~

For those who practise it bird-watching is not only a sport and a science, but also something near a religion, and after all its externals have been inventoried the essence stays incommunicable.

BRITISH ORNITHOLOGIST AND ENVIRONMENTALIST
MAX NICHOLSON, WHO FOUNDED THE BRITISH TRUST FOR
ORNITHOLOGY (BTO) IN 1938

~~~~~~~~~~~~~~~~

Why do gulls flock to airports and cause alarm for pilots?

Gulls like flat, open terrain to roost so that they can spot predators more easily, making airports and small airfields an ideal habitat for them to set up home. This can be a major problem for aircraft pilots, especially if the birds are taking off or landing in large groups. Pelicans, ducks, swans, egrets and herons also cause problems to airline traffic around the globe, delaying flights and causing often severe and costly damage to engines. It is estimated that between 200 and 500

Birding slang

LBJ – Little Brown Job. Hundreds of birds are small and brown, making identification difficult.

BOP – bird of prey.

Dude – a fair-weather, often well-off elderly birder who knows little about birds but just enjoys a nice day out with nature from time to time. A dude doesn't know his grebes from his grouse but he's harmless and infinitely better company than a know-all twitcher.

Dip out on – fail to see the bird the watcher has made a special effort to come and see.

Tick – a species new to a birdwatcher's list. Literally, ticking off the species in a notebook.

Megatick – spotting a very rare bird.

Crippler – one up from a megatick because it leaves the watcher emotionally crippled by its beauty as well as its rarity. (Some birds, no matter how rare, are still LBJs. See above.)

Sibe – a bird from Siberia that has got lost during migration.

Sum plum – summer plumage.

Twitcher – obsessive birdwatcher prepared to travel hundreds of miles for a possible sighting of a rare bird. The trainspotters people have been killed in plane crashes caused by bird strike in the last 20 years alone. Airports go to great lengths to deter the birds and most strip away as much vegetation as possible, especially trees where birds can roost. Devices to make loud noises, bright lights, patrol dogs and shotguns are all used to good effect.

of the birdwatching world, twitchers are more interested in ticking off all the species than admiring the beauty of the creatures they go to such lengths to see. The term has come to be applied to anyone who watches birds, to the annoyance of the less obsessive ones or 'birders' as they prefer to be known.

Grip someone off – see a bird that someone in the group didn't. A source of tremendous satisfaction to twitchers who enjoy nothing more than getting one over a rival know-all, seen-all bore. It is not unknown for a twitcher to pass on deliberate misinformation or, in extreme cases, even scare a bird away so that no one else sees it.

Vis mig – visible migration. Seeing a bird on the move, taking part in one of nature's most mysterious phenomena, can be a very emotional experience. The birds will often be at the beginning or end of a journey lasting weeks and months and covering thousands of miles, and seeing them is akin to saying 'farewell' or 'welcome back' to an old friend.

Seawatching – an experience that often numbs the body with cold and the mind with boredom, perched for a whole day on a windswept cliff or rocky outcrop in the hope of seeing a rare seabird. Hugely rewarding if one is spotted but this is an activity generally only practised by the extremely committed and/or the extremely unhinged.

One for sorrow
Two for joy
Three for a wedding
Four for a boy
Five for silver
Six for gold
Seven for a secret never to be told
Eight for heaven
Nine for hell
And ten for the devil's own self.

VERSION OF TRADITIONAL RHYME ABOUT SEEING MAGPIES (ALSO SAID OF CROWS, THE MAGPIES' COUSINS)

Birds as bombs

Genghis Khan used birds as incendiary bombs when his Mongol hordes laid siege to the city of Volohoi in the early thirteenth century. Unable to breach the defences by more conventional means, the Mongol emperor tricked the inhabitants of the largely wooden city by offering peace in return for their gift of thousands of swallows and cats. His troops then fixed strips of burning cloth to the cats and birds and released them at the city's edge. Many of the flaming creatures fled back into the city, setting dozens of buildings on fire. In the pandemonium that followed, the Khan's army were able to breach the defences and overrun the city.

Why don't people eat crow?

'To eat crow' is an old expression with the same meaning as 'to eat humble pie': to admit being wrong. But many people used to eat crow, because it was a perfectly acceptable alternative to fancier game meats. It was not a rich man's dish, but those who have tried it say it tastes a little like duck and the darkest meat of chicken. Rooks, starlings and dunlin (in coastal areas) were also eaten in rural households up until tinned foods became widely available in the early twentieth century. Like most birds, crows have no white meat on them and, being scrawnier beasts than domestic fowl, with most of the meat on the breast, you will need several to make a meal. Cook the breasts as you would chicken. If one of the local guns ever offers you a couple of brace of *Corvus corone*, whip up the following simple recipe and impress your friends and family with your resourcefulness.

Pan-fried crow breast in breadcrumbs

Remove the breast meat from the carcasses and tenderize it with a meat mallet. Dunk the pieces in beaten egg and then into breadcrumbs or a spiced flour mixture. Fry them with some bacon in hot oil, turning them over at least once. Connoisseurs say the middle should have a touch of pink.

> And these are they which ye shall have in abomination among the fowls; they shall not be eaten, they are an abomination: the eagle, and the ossifrage, and the ospray, and the vulture, and the kite after his kind; every raven after his kind; and the owl, and the night hawk, and the cuckow, and the hawk after his kind, and the little owl, and the cormorant, and the great owl, and the swan, and the pelican, and the gier eagle, and the stork, the heron after her kind, and the lapwing, and the bat.
>
> **Leviticus 11:13–19**

The capercaillie, a large woodland grouse threatened with extinction in the UK, lives off young pine-needles in its native Scottish forests. The meat of the bird, flavoured by the needles, is said to taste like turpentine and is virtually uneatable. In Sweden, where this eccentric-looking bird is still found in great numbers, it is the tradition to soak the bird in sour milk to get rid of its foul tang. In Scotland they used to bury it for the same reason.

Bird phrases

Swan song
Pecking order
Ugly duckling
Give the bird
Birdbrain
Bird's nest
Stool pigeon
Sitting duck
Cockney sparrow
Penguin suit
For the birds
Up with the lark
Duck (cricket score)
Chicken out
Spring chicken
Birds and the bees
Bird's-eye view
Lame duck
Hen party
Night owl
Cold turkey
Take under your wing
Ruffle someone's
  feathers
Home bird
Rare bird
A dead duck
Cook somebody's goose
Have goose pimples
Wild goose chase

Waiter, I think someone's spat in my soup

The principal ingredient of the Chinese dish bird's nest soup is the saliva of a swiftlet, or cave swift, found in southern Asia and the islands of the Pacific. The swifts build their cup-shaped nests using saliva, which hardens when it dries. When dissolved in hot water the nests create a thick, gelatinous mixture, which is rich in nutrients and supposedly helpful in relieving a wide range of health problems – including asthma and poor digestion – and boosting the immune system and libido.

The nests were once harvested in the wild but today they are taken from concrete structures built specifically to attract flocks of the swifts. Bird's nest soup is a growing, highly lucrative industry serving restaurants in China, Hong Kong and New York where customers will pay up to $100 for a bowl.

❝English Sparrows are being properly appreciated. Hundreds of them are now caught by enterprising people for sale to certain restaurants where reed birds are in demand. A German woman on Third Avenue has three traps set every day, and she catches probably seventy-five a week. They are cooked and served to her boarders the same as reed birds and are declared quite as great a delicacy. This German woman bastes them, leaving the little wooden skewer in the bird when served. They are cooked with a bit of bacon . . . The females are the choice meat. The males can be told by the circle of white feathers at the neck. The females are as plain as Quakeresses . . . Sparrow pie is a delicacy fit to set before a king. ❞

NEW YORK TIMES, 20 JULY 1887

GOLDEN RULES FOR FEEDING BIRDS

- Never feed salty foods to birds. A bird can't digest salt and it will damage its nervous system.

- Put out only the quantity that can be eaten in one day – or you risk attracting mice and rats.

- Make sure you provide birds with water as well. They need to drink (and wash).

- Be mindful of hygiene risk; wash your hands thoroughly after filling feeders and bird baths and wear gloves when you scrub them out. Let them dry before refilling to kill off harmful bacteria and prevent mould build-up.

- Place feeders and tables in positions safe from ambush by cats, and not too close to house windows. If birds don't like where you've put them, they simply won't come. Move the feeders around until the birds arrive.

- Wash out and fill up bird baths almost daily in summer.

- Keep tables and areas beneath feeders clear of droppings, which quickly become infected with hazardous bacteria and diseases.

Sparrow pie was a common dish in Britain until the First World War, and songbirds such as the blackbird and the thrush have been a delicacy on mainland Europe for centuries. They were particularly popular in autumn after the birds had gorged themselves on ripened grapes. Dutch Customs officials made a number of spectacular finds in the 1990s, seizing consignments from China containing millions of plucked frozen sparrows, en route to Italy, highlighting that there is still great appetite for small wild birds.

> ❛There are instances in which the eating of birds' flesh may react unfavourably upon the human system. The hard meat of the wood pigeon (*Columba palumbus*), for example, is extremely binding and gamekeepers and other countrymen, eating a great many of them, have been seriously affected. The flesh of green pigeons of the genus *Treron*, after they have been eating figs, will turn the urine of the eater bright green, which has no harmful effect other than temporary alarm. ❜
>
> **M. F. M. MEIKLEJOHN (1870–1963),** *WILD BIRDS AS HUMAN FOOD*

A leading figure in the Scottish Ornithologists' Club, Meiklejohn became a bird lover when he returned from the Boer War where he distinguished himself as a captain in the Gordon Highlanders. He was awarded the Victoria Cross for his valour at the Battle of Elandslaagte in October 1899 when, according to his citation, after his troops were caught in a heavy crossfire, 'he rallied the men and led them against the enemy's position, where he fell, desperately wounded in four places'.

Chicken, duck, goose and quail eggs are not the only ones fit to be eaten. Gulls' eggs are a delicacy in Britain and Scandinavia and pheasant eggs are especially delicious if poached and served with a Hollandaise sauce. The law prohibits collecting and selling wild birds' eggs, but licences can be obtained to hunt for certain types of eggs (gulls' mainly) for limited periods of the year.

BIRDS AND THE LAW

All birds, their nests and eggs are protected by law. With a small handful of exceptions, it is an offence to intentionally:

- kill, injure or take any wild bird;

- take, damage or destroy the nest of any wild bird while it is in use or being built;

- take or destroy the egg of any wild bird;

- disturb any listed wild bird while it is nest building, or at a nest containing eggs or young, or disturb the dependent young of such a bird.

Contrary to his depiction as a gentle character in the classic 1962 film that bears his name, the Birdman of Alcatraz was a violent bully loathed by his fellow inmates in the various prisons where he spent his entire adult life. Robert Stroud ran away from home at 13 and within five years he was working as a pimp in Alaska. He was jailed for 12 years after shooting dead an acquaintance who had beaten Gould's prostitute girlfriend. After stabbing a fellow prisoner, he was transferred to Leavenworth Prison in Kansas in 1912, where he began to educate himself through university extension courses, taking a particular interest in ornithology. In 1916 he took time off from his studies to stab and kill a guard. He was sentenced to hang, but following a plea from his mother, President Woodrow Wilson commuted his sentence to life imprisonment in solitary confinement. It was then, with no humans to befriend, shoot or stab, that he began raising and studying birds. Some of his research was smuggled out of prison and published in his book *Stroud's Digest on the Diseases of Birds* (1943), which became an important work of its time in its field. In 1942 he was transferred to Alcatraz, the prison island off San Francisco, where he was allowed to continue his studies but was barred from further publishing ventures. He died in 1963 with no friends or admirers, but there was nothing he couldn't tell you about avian pathology.

The Canary Islands were named after the wild Mastiff-like dogs that lived there, and not for the birds of the same name, as is commonly supposed. The Romans gave Gran Canaria, the largest of this string of Atlantic islands, the name Canaria Insula, meaning Island of the Dogs.

How the starlings conquered America

Africa's red-billed quelea is probably the world's most populous bird, but the starling comes in a close second. Today, the starling is a common sight in the United States where their numbers have grown exponentially since they were introduced from Europe at the end of the nineteenth century by Eugene Schieffelin, an eccentric millionaire drug manufacturer. Schieffelin wanted every songbird mentioned in the plays of William Shakespeare to be enjoyed by New Yorkers, but he was unsuccessful with attempts to introduce skylarks, chaffinches and song thrushes. The starling, however, is one of the world's hardiest, most adaptable birds and quickly found a niche for itself in the local ecology. Schieffelin released 100 of them in Central Park in 1890. Within a hundred years there were 250 million of them living in the States.

❝ The eggs of the turkey are almost as mild as those of the hen; the egg of the goose is large, but well-tasted. Duck's eggs have a rich flavour; the albumen is slightly transparent, or bluish, when set or coagulated by boiling, which requires less time than hen's eggs. Guinea-fowl eggs are smaller and more delicate than those of the hen. Eggs of wild fowl are generally coloured, often spotted; and the taste generally partakes somewhat of the flavour of the bird they belong to. Those of land birds that are eaten, as the plover, lapwing, ruff, &c., are in general much esteemed; but those of sea-fowl have, more or less, a strong fishy taste. ❞

MRS BEETON (1836–65)

A BEGINNER'S GUIDE TO BIRDWATCHING

- Get a good identification book. There are lots to choose from today.

- Buy a pair of binoculars (7x or 8x magnification are the best). There are perfectly good ones for under £30.

- Start in your garden or local park. If you know any experienced birdwatchers, try to spend a day with them to learn some tips.

- Buy a birdsong CD so you can start to learn the songs and calls of some of the most common species.

- Join a local birdwatching club. Sign up to the RSPB or BTO, both outstanding in their fields, so to speak.

- To see a variety of species seek out the best sites near to you, including woodland, meadows, estuaries, coast-lines, riverbanks and lakes.

- Read up on the behaviour of birds to learn where and at what time of the day or year you are most likely to see them.

- Buy an alarm clock. It's often just after daybreak when birds are at their most active, especially in the breeding season with so many extra mouths to feed.

- When you feel confident enough to leave your garden and start venturing further afield, wear dull, natural colours, or better still camouflage clothing, to blend in with your surroundings.

- Always find a bird with your naked eye first. It's no good searching with your 'bins' because the field of vision is too narrow.

Why are so many gulls found living inland these days?

Some claim that the influx of herring and lesser black-backed gulls began during a run of cold winters in the late nineteenth century when factory workers took pity on them and fed them scraps in their lunch breaks. Today, food remains the main reason why tens of thousands of them have abandoned their former homes on the cliffs of our coastline and headed into town to live. These gulls must rank among the most unpopular in Britain owing to the din of their squawking, the fouling of public places with droppings, the great expense of clearing up after them, the tearing open of rubbish bags in the search for scraps, the aggressive defence of their young in the breeding season and their ability to steal an ice cream or a fish supper straight out of our hands. But the gull's defenders say we humans only have ourselves to blame for what is becoming a major problem for a number of towns. Firstly, they say there wouldn't be an urban gull problem if it weren't for our habit of leaving our rubbish lying around in our streets and in giant landfill sites. Secondly, our devastation of marine fish stocks has played havoc with the feeding habits of our coastal birds. Gulls used to scavenge behind trawlers, but decades of overfishing has led to a huge reduction in commercial operations with the result that there are far fewer vessels at sea. Moreover, the offal of the gutted fish, that was once thrown overboard and snaffled by the gulls, has been kept in recent years for the production of fish meal, allowing hard-up fishermen to make a few extra quid. As these sources of food began to disappear, the ever resourceful and intelligent gulls turned to the land to forage and were delighted to discover that our tall urban buildings with their flat rooftops were not just considerably warmer than their old wind-blasted cliff-faces, but they were even safer from foxes and other predators. The number of gulls nesting on roofs has quadrupled in the last 15 years, bringing them into conflict with the human inhabitants and creating a headache for local councils who are unable to act because these gulls are currently listed as species of conservation concern.

from **Home Thoughts, from Abroad**

And after April, when May follows,
And the whitethroat builds, and all the swallows!
Hark, where my blossom'd pear-tree in the hedge
Leans to the field and scatters on the clover
Blossoms and dewdrops – at the bent spray's edge –
That's the wise thrush; he sings each song twice over,
Lest you should think he never could recapture
The first fine careless rapture!
And though the fields look rough with hoary dew,
All will be gay when noontide wakes anew
The buttercups, the little children's dower
– Far brighter than this gaudy melon-flower!

ROBERT BROWNING (1812–89)

Pigeons: war heroes to zeroes

Today, an email message clicks into our inbox with a piece of important information; 100 years ago a pigeon fluttered back into its roost with the news tied to its body. As soon as man discovered that a pigeon had the ability to return to its nest from hundreds of miles away, he began to use the bird as a means of long-distance communication. We know pigeons were widely used by Greeks and Romans for a whole host of purposes, from passing back vital military information to sending personal letters and delivering the results of the Olympic Games. In the Middle Ages, the cities of the Middle East were all linked by an extensive network of pigeon post. At the turn of the twentieth century, English football fans smuggled birds into away football matches and released them at half-time and the final whistle to fly home and inform the locals of the score. Pigeons played an important role in the two World Wars, saving thousands of lives in conflicts, carrying messages back from soldiers and undercover agents behind enemy lines. In the First World War they often flew through heavy bombardment and poison gas to deliver vital information. The birds were also released from convoy ships in the

Atlantic after a U-boat torpedo attack, giving the coordinates of the location of the sinking ship so that the crew might be rescued. Today, pigeons are no longer cherished and admired as they were for so many centuries. On the contrary, they are regarded as an unhygienic nuisance and millions of them are exterminated every year across the globe by pest controllers.

Goose-stepping army reaches London

For hundreds of years, until the late nineteenth century, huge flocks of geese, reared mainly in East Anglia, were marched to London markets after having their feet dipped in tar and sand to help them on their long journey. (Turkeys were fitted with little leather boots for their comfort.) The goose was a very important feature in households of the day, providing eggs and meat to eat, feathers for quills, pillows and cushions and fat for cooking as well as for use as a dry-skin cream and a cure for chest and throat complaints when mixed with honey. Today, goose feathers are still used in a wide variety of products, including bedding, natural toothpicks and badminton shuttlecocks.

No goose before or since has achieved such celebrity as a gander called Old Tom, whose death after 37 years of living in London's Leadenhall Market was reported at great length in *The Times* on 16 April 1835. Old Tom had become a favourite among traders and cus-

tomers alike in the market after he emerged a lone survivor from the slaughter of 34,000 geese. Following his death he was embalmed and lay in state, his body guarded by two other geese, and hundreds of Londoners flocked to pay their respects, each of them handing over a penny for the privilege. The money raised went towards a grave and headstone in Leadenhall Market, the inscription declaring Old Tom to be 'The chief of geese, the poulterer's pride'.

Eco-thieves target rare birds

The caged-bird trade is very good business for crooks and very bad news for nature lovers – not to mention the birds themselves. The sharp decline in many exotic bird species can be laid at the door of the smugglers. Roughly a third of the world's most endangered species are threatened by human interference and exploitation. The plundering of wild populations is concentrated mainly in the South American rainforest (what's left of it) and China, Indonesia and the

Philippines, but the birds, many of which die during capture or in transit, are sold in countries across the world, including Britain and the United States. Songbirds, such as finches, warblers and weavers, are hunted and traded, but their value is low and the big money comes from the more exotic, colourful birds of the parrot family such as macaws, Amazons, cockatoos, lovebirds, parakeets, mynahs and toucans. It is virtually impossible to obtain reliable figures from this nefarious, murky world, but conservative estimates suggest that roughly two million birds are sold every year.

> Stork, stork, fly away,
> Stand not on one leg, I pray,
> See your wife is in her nest,
> With her little ones at rest.
> They will hang one,
> And fry another;
> They will shoot a third,
> And roast his brother.
> **HANS CHRISTIAN ANDERSEN (1805–75)**

❝About one thing the Englishman has a particularly strict code. If a bird says *Cluk bik bik bik bik* and *caw* you may kill it, eat it, or ask Fortnums to pickle it in Napoleon brandy with wild strawberries. If it says *tweet* it is a dear and precious friend and you'd better lay off it if you want to remain a member of Boodles. ❞

ENGLISH WRITER AND BROADCASTER CLEMENT FREUD (1924 –)

HOW TO HELP YOUR BIRDS IN WINTER

Winter is a difficult time of year for birds. The days are short, there is less time to feed and the nights are cold, which means they must eat a lot more food if they are to have the energy to keep warm and survive until the morning. As if that wasn't enough, food is harder for them to find in winter. Most insects are hibernating, worms are harder to extract from the colder earth, and snow and ice can make it even more difficult. Feeding birds the leftovers from your kitchen will help many of them to survive into spring, but be careful what you give them.

What to feed birds from your kitchen in winter:

- Cold boiled **potatoes** or roast potatoes, opened up.

- Cold cooked **root vegetables** such as carrots and parsnips.

- Cut-up **apples and pears** are gratefully received even if they're a little bruised or on the turn. Dried fruits, such as currants, sultanas and raisins, are popular too.

- Pieces of mild to medium strength **hard cheese** like cheddar are popular with many birds including robins, blackbirds and song thrushes. Wrens like it too but for them to take it you have to place it near the hedgerows where they skulk.

- **Fat** from cuts of unsalted meat can be laid out in large slices. Secure them to the ground or bird table with a heavy object to stop larger birds flying away with the entire piece.

- Old **cake** and broken **biscuit** are a welcome treat, being high in fat.

Don't make the mistake of feeding salted foods as birds can't digest them and they may damage their nervous system. Don't provide soft fats such as polyunsaturated margarines and vegetable oils as these can destroy the waterproofing and insulating qualities of feathers.

The Majesty of Flight

HOW AND WHY BIRDS FLY

Happier of happy though I be like them
I cannot take possession of the sky,
Mount with a thoughtless impulse, and wheel there,
One of a mighty multitude whose way and motion is a harmony
and dance
Magnificent.

ENGLISH POET WILLIAM WORDSWORTH (1770–1850)

Why did birds start to fly?

We don't know for sure but one theory is that birds' ancestors –
dinosaurs that resembled running lizards – leaped higher and higher
over a period of millions of years as they ran to catch insects, flapping
their feathered arms for extra propulsion. This is called the 'Ground-
up' theory. The more credible theory is that these ancient creatures
had much in common with the flying squirrels and lizards alive today,
climbing trees with their sharp-clawed hind feet and then gliding
back down to the ground. That way the creature saved energy by not
having to scuttle down one tree before running up another. It was
then just a short evolutionary step, albeit one that went on
for tens of millions of years, to start gliding from branch to
branch, tree to tree; then on to the next stage of flying
longer distances. This is known as the 'Trees-
down' hypothesis. As for why they might
want to go up trees in the first place,
much of the world was carpeted
in forest way back in prehis-
tory and creatures learned to
climb trees for a number of reasons, including to lay eggs, to feed
off insects and to escape predators.

Dawn
Ecstatic bird songs pound
the hollow vastness of the sky
with metallic clinkings –
beating color up into it
at a far edge,– beating it, beating it
with rising, triumphant ardor, –
stirring it into warmth,
quickening in it a spreading change, –
bursting wildly against it as
dividing the horizon, a heavy sun
lifts himself – is lifted –
bit by bit above the edge
of things, – -runs free at last
out into the open – !lumbering
glorified in full release upward –
  songs cease.
US POET WILLIAM CARLOS WILLIAMS (1883–1963)

The magic of flight

So accustomed are we to the sight of a bird in flight that we have
ceased to be amazed by it, but how evolution has allowed an animal
to achieve mastery of the air is one of the great marvels of nature.
The bird's extraordinary body has been designed to minute specifications in order that it may rise above the rest of the animal world
and live life on the wing. Humans couldn't have devised a better
flying machine if they had spent tens of millions of years in the effort.

The bird has become by far the lightest animal in relation to its
size in order that it may fly. (Flightless birds such as penguins and
ostriches are very heavy because they no longer need to get airborne.)
The bird doesn't have a heavy tail to drag around, nor any teeth,
while its reproductive organs, male and female, shrink to virtual non-
existence outside the breeding season. Bone-matter is heavy so
evolution has got rid of as much of it as it can – over millions of
years, of course – by eliminating some bones altogether, fusing others
and hollowing out those that remain, filling them with air for added
buoyancy.

In order to meet the enormous demands imposed by flying on the metabolism, a bird has the most efficient breathing system in the animal kingdom. It has a four-chambered heart, just as a human does, but proportionately the heart weighs six times more and its beat is incredibly rapid. The resting heart rate of a small garden bird is about 500 beats per minute while its respiratory system takes up 20 per cent of its body volume compared with 5 per cent in humans. A bird has a series of air sacs throughout its body (nine in most species) that are connected to its two lungs and its hollow bones. The sacs in the back are called the 'posterior' and those in the front of the body the 'anterior' air sacs. Evolution has devised a highly resourceful system that passes the air in a one-way, staggered flow through the bird's lungs, providing a constant supply of fresh oxygen-rich air. When a bird inhales through the nostrils at the base of its beak, the air passes first into the posterior air sacs and then, when it breathes out, into the lungs. When the next breath is inhaled into the posterior sacs, the air from the first moves from the lungs into the anterior air sacs. When it exhales again, the air from the first breath is expelled from the bird, while the second breath travels into the lungs and so on ...

The way a human breathes is not especially efficient but it's good enough to allow us to go about our daily business of clubbing each other, running away from woolly mammoths, playing football and so forth. We absorb just 20 per cent of the oxygen from each breath whereas a bird absorbs 100 per cent thanks to its network of air sacs.

As a finishing touch, the bird's streamlined plumage minimizes air resistance, improves aerodynamics and reduces the amount of energy needed to move through the air.

The birds that don't fly, or aren't very good at it, evolved from efficient flying ancestors to suit specific ecological niches.

Golden eagles often hunt in pairs. One flies over the contours of the land, flushing out alarmed prey, which, if all goes to plan, rears up straight into the talons of the second bird. Eagles are seriously impressive hunters with a host of techniques. They can spot a hare from over a mile away and plunge straight down from a great height to take it.

The Dalliance of the Eagles

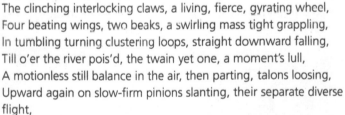

Skirting the river road, (my forenoon walk, my rest,)
Skyward in air a sudden muffled sound, the dalliance of the eagles,
The rushing amorous contact high in space together,
The clinching interlocking claws, a living, fierce, gyrating wheel,
Four beating wings, two beaks, a swirling mass tight grappling,
In tumbling turning clustering loops, straight downward falling,
Till o'er the river pois'd, the twain yet one, a moment's lull,
A motionless still balance in the air, then parting, talons loosing,
Upward again on slow-firm pinions slanting, their separate diverse flight,
She hers, he his, pursuing.

US POET WALT WHITMAN (1819–92)

Why do you never see a swift sitting down?

Like the hummingbird, another extraordinarily adept flier, the swift is virtually incapable of walking. It is the evolutionary price it has paid for its spectacular aerial skills. Both species of bird belong to the order known as Apodiformes, from the Greek meaning 'footless'. The swift is so bad at walking that it's more stable if it clings to a vertical surface than it is on level ground.

The swift is even more useless on terra firma than the virtually legless shearwater and will never land on the ground deliberately. If it is blown there in severe weather or collapses after an arduous migration, it struggles to get airborne again and is extremely vulnerable to predators. The only time the swift settles on solid matter is when, during the breeding season, it returns to the nest it has built from grass, feathers and spittle, either in a hole in a cliff or in the loft of a house. For the other nine or so months of the year, the swift is in the air. It eats in the air, mouth open like a basking shark, surviving entirely on a diet of insects; it drinks in the air, skimming the surface of a pond or a lake, and possibly by consuming raindrops too. The swift even mates on the wing, the male landing on the female's back for a couple of seconds. But the prize for the bird with the greatest number of continuous flying hours must surely go to the sooty tern, which remains airborne from the moment it has fledged until it starts breeding, a full six years later at the earliest.

The shearwater, meanwhile, is so adapted to the aquatic life that its legs have effectively become worthless stubs. They are positioned so far back on its body that it can barely stand up or walk, forcing it instead to shuffle along on its belly. This shortcoming makes it vulnerable to predators so it nests in a burrow in the ground and it comes ashore only at night.

Nature's fastest creatures

Flying is an incredibly efficient way of moving: a human sprinter can run the equivalent of between 5 and 7 lengths of his own body per second; a cheetah, the fastest animal, can cover 16 to 18; but a bird can move at about 75 body lengths per second, making it as fast as a jet plane in relation to its size.

Why is it that millions of birds in huge swirling flocks never collide?

This question has fascinated scientists and bird-watchers for centuries, and it is only recently that they have got close to solving the mystery. Ornithologists call the mass simultaneous gyration of birds the 'chorus-line effect'. In Britain we have starlings to lay on these spectacular aerial entertainments, but following a 70 per cent crash in the numbers of these once ubiquitous birds over the past 40 years the displays are not as common as they once were. It used to be thought that a leader bird was somehow choreographing the show, perhaps by transmitting commands through some mysterious, extrasensory means that only birds could understand. But scientists have recently worked out that each bird takes its cue from the bird next to it and acts on it almost instantaneously, just like a Mexican wave inside a stadium. As flocks grow in size, the speed of the twists and turns and wheeling increases, leading to the spectacular display we see  when over a million starlings congregate at the end of the day before heading off to their communal roost. But we still don't know *why* they do it.

The Woodlark

Teevo cheevo cheevio chee:
O where, what can thát be?
Weedio-weedio: there again!
So tiny a trickle of sóng-strain
And all round not to be found
For brier, bough, furrow, or gréen ground
Before or behind or far or at hand
Either left either right
Anywhere in the súnlight.
Well, after all! Ah but hark –
'I am the little wóodlark.

Today the sky is two and two
With white strokes and strains of the blue

Round a ring, around a ring
And while I sail (must listen) I sing

The skylark is my cousin and he
Is known to men more than me

. . . when the cry within
Says Go on then I go on
Till the longing is less and the good gone

But down drop, if it says Stop,
To the all-a-leaf of the tréetop
And after that off the bough

I ám so véry, O só very glád
That I dó thínk there is not to be had

The blue wheat-acre is underneath
And the corn is corded and shoulders its sheaf,
The ear in milk, lush the sash,
And crush-silk poppies aflash,
The blood-gush blade-gash
Flame-rash rudred
Bud shelling or broad-shed
Tatter-tangled and dingle-a-dangled
Dandy-hung dainty head.

And down . . . the furrow dry
Sunspurge and oxeye
And lace-leaved lovely
Foam-tuft fumitory

Through the velvety wind V-winged
To the nest's nook I balance and buoy
With a sweet joy of a sweet joy,
Sweet, of a sweet, of a sweet joy
Of a sweet – a sweet – sweet – joy.'

GERARD MANLEY HOPKINS

Flocking hell

Red-billed queleas live in massive flocks of over a million birds, which can take up to six hours to pass overhead, descending like a Biblical plague and stripping fields of crops bare within minutes. The avian equivalent of locusts, they are mainly a problem in east Africa, the world's worst drought and famine zone, and it is during the dry season, when food sources are limited, that the birds present the biggest threat. In the wet season, there's plenty of grass seed for them to feed on, but for the rest of the year they must seek out other sources. Over the past few decades, farmers and governments, supported by armies, have tried everything to thwart the quelea – including petrol bombs, dynamite and flame-throwers – but without success. Like cockroaches and rats, they will not be stamped out.

~~~~~~~~~~~~~~~~~~~~~~~~~~~~~~

To a man, ornithologists are tall, slender,
and bearded so that they can stand motionless
for hours, imitating kindly trees, as they
watch for birds.

US WRITER GORE VIDAL (1925–)

~~~~~~~~~~~~~~~~~~~~~~~~~~~~~~

Why are chickens and pheasants rubbish at flying?

A bad-tempered scientist with haemorrhoids running to catch a train might well bark: 'It is to do with dietary behaviour, natural selection and low-aspect-ratio wings in relation to body mass, you bloody imbecile!' and barge past you. But it's nothing to get worked up about – toss another log on the fire and sit back. Pheasants and chickens belong to an order of bird known as Galliformes, characterized by plump bodies, short wide wings and reasonably long legs. When you chase one, it will run away and will only take to the air if, say, it was being chased by Bernard Matthews and it was a choice between escaping into the nearest tree or ending up as some kind of 'medallion' or 'twizzler' drowning in a pool of spaghetti hoops on the plate of an unhappy five-year-old.

Many domesticated Galliformes, including gamebirds reared for shooting, have been stuffed with so much feed they either can't fly at all or can get only a few feet off the ground. Their cousins in the wild actually aren't a great deal more adept, because they have evolved to scavenge for their food in undergrowth and on forest floors. In their original habitats, all they needed to escape the attentions of a land predator was the ability to fly as far as the nearest branch. Efficient flying was not a skill they needed to survive, hence the ungainly, explosive flapping to lift their bulky frames off the ground. Like a rower being forced to propel himself with short, stubby oars, the game bird can flap as much as it likes but it's not going to get very far.

Contrast the wings of a pheasant with those of a seabird or a long-distance wader and you will understand the difference in flying ability. Seabirds like the albatross, and other good long-distance fliers, have long, narrow, pointed wings which allow them to ride strong winds and glide at high speed with barely any effort. The vulture's wings are also long but they are wider than those of the albatross because vultures soar at lower speeds to spot sources of food. Indeed, the shape of a bird's wings tells you exactly what kind of bird it is and the life it leads: the hummingbird's are designed for hovering, those of the swallow, swift and martin for acrobatics, while your average garden bird has short, elliptical-shaped wings for quick take-off and manoeuvring within the tight confines of woods and shrubbery. For game birds that spend most of the time on the ground flying is just a last resort.

Penguins prefer to swim

The penguin surrendered its power of flight over time, swapping it for an ability to dive and swim as it slowly transformed itself into an aquatic bird that lives off marine food, rather than insects, plants or meat. Today, some species spend as much as 80 per cent of their lives in the wet stuff. The penguin's wings have become flippers and the light, hollow bones characteristic of a flighted bird have been replaced by heavy, dense ones to reduce buoyancy (as has happened in other birds who dive underwater to find food). The penguin has become so good at swimming that it can outpace and outmanoeuvre many fish. The most impressive swimmer of them all, the Michael Phelps of the avian world, is the emperor penguin, that can stay underwater for a quarter of an hour, plunge to depths of 500 metres and travel up to 600 miles in a single trip in search of food.

In-flight water purifying system

Albatrosses, storm petrels and shearwaters belong to a group of seabirds known as tubenoses, so called after the shape of their specially adapted nasal glands and nostril tubes which allow them to expel the salt from the seawater they drink. The ability to drink at sea means the birds can live above the oceans for months, even years at a time, without having to touch land. Given a choice, however, they will choose fresh water over seawater.

How does a bird actually fly?

There are two forces of nature that a bird – and an aeroplane – must get the better of in order to fly: gravity and drag. While gravity pulls an object to the ground, drag resists its forward movement through the air. To overcome this twin resistance a bird must generate one force known as lift, that propels it clear of the ground, and another force known as thrust, to drive it through the air. Small birds are light enough to flap their wings and take off from a standing start but heavier birds such as ground-dwelling ducks, with their more solid bones and thicker plumage, need to run, or flap over the surface of the water, to generate enough forward momentum to carry them upwards, just as an aeroplane has to hurtle down a runway. Swans and bustards, the largest flying birds, need an even longer run-up and have to put in an even greater effort.

How a bird stays airborne is slightly more complicated and the following includes no more than an elementary outline of the biology and physics involved. The thrust to drive it through the air is generated by powerful flight muscles attached to its keel, an extension of the sternum, which acts as an anchor. The shape of the wing holds the key to maintaining the balance between lift and drag as the bird flaps, soars and glides.

The cross-section of a bird's wing is almost identical to that of an aeroplane and both operate according to similar aerodynamic principles. Slice a wing in half and, side on, it looks like a teardrop. Air moving across the aerofoil shape provides the necessary lift, as the pressure above the wing drops and increases below it. So long as the lift is greater than the weight of the bird and the drag caused by air resistance, the bird will stay in the air. Some birds also have a feature on each wing called an alula, which acts in the same way as the

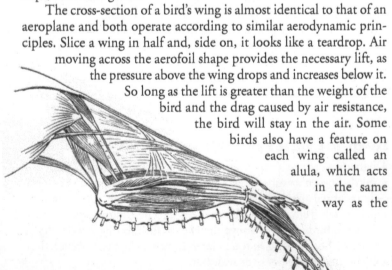

flaps on a plane wing, helping the bird to counteract the increasing drag and thus stay airborne when moving at slower speeds, for instance, when it comes in to land.

Why do geese fly in a V formation and not a B or K formation?

Not, as the village idiots in my local pub suggested, because the one at the front is the only one that knows where it's going or because birds aren't very good at reading. Many species, notably geese, ducks and pelicans, fly in V formation because it improves aerodynamics and helps save energy on long journeys, allowing them to travel many

hundreds or even thousands of miles further than if they flew alone, or in a different formation. The birds take advantage of the air turbulence by positioning themselves near the tips of their neighbour's wings, all flapping their wings in time with the leader and riding on the upwash generated by the downward stroke of the wing. It's a similar principle to that of the moving boat which leaves smoother water behind its V-shaped wake. The leading bird at the point of the V has to make the greatest effort because it encounters the most air resistance, which explains why the birds take it in turns to hold that position.

Why do birds of a feather flock together?

Roughly half of the world's 10,000 bird species congregate in flocks at some time or other in spite of the risk of catastrophic annihilation caused by disease, a freak weather event or a mob of human beings armed with guns and nets. They do so for many of the same reasons that seabirds live in colonies – because the benefits for an individual bird of being in a community outweigh those of living alone. The odds

IN THE GARDEN
Working the bins

Even for the casual bird lover who has no intention of straying further than the end of the garden, buying a pair of half-decent binoculars, or 'bins', will prove a worthwhile investment. Being flighty, jumpy creatures, birds tend to take to the air or retreat into the shrubbery at the first rustle of the undergrowth or crunch of a boot. Cocksure robins, sparrows and blackbirds, as well as wood pigeons, collared doves and piratical magpies, will be slower to retreat, but with most other species it's difficult to get up close to observe their fascinating behaviour and mannerisms. A pair of bins will open up a whole new appreciation of how birds go about their daily struggle to survive. It's one thing to watch a bird pecking away at a peanut feeder, quite another to watch one busily flying back and forth to build a nest or singing from the treetops to attract a mate.

The very best binoculars cost over £1,000, but there are perfectly adequate pairs available for under £50 and even better quality second-hand ones to be had for even less.

It's important to get the magnification right and not be tempted to go for the ones with the biggest numbers. The specification is given as two numbers with a cross between of being snatched by a predator become longer with every addition to the flock, while finding food is easier if there are more individuals on the lookout for it.

It's not always birds of the same feather that flock together because the urgency to eat transcends the species. Sparrows and starlings hunt for food in a flock all year round, but when food becomes scarce in the winter months, less gregarious birds, such as finches and tits, will also team up to seek out sources, leading to

---

them (e.g. 8x30 or 7x20). The first number refers to the power of magnification, so an 8x pair will make objects look eight times closer. Birdwatchers, however experienced, don't want the magnification to be any greater than x7 or x8 as it's difficult to keep the image stable. Forget zoom binoculars too as they don't admit enough light. The second number in the specification is the width in millimetres of the largest lens, known as the objective lens, and the larger it is the more light it lets in, making it more effective in dull weather, and at sunrise and dusk. The drawback is that the bigger the lens the heavier it is to hold, which is a consideration to bear in mind as it can be tiring to hold the arms in the binoculars position for long periods of time.

You are also better off buying a pair with a focusing wheel that doesn't need much turning to secure a quick, clear image either long-range or close up. You'll need to be fast on the draw sometimes as many birds tend not to hang around. Don't buy binoculars you haven't tried because different pairs suit different eye sockets. You don't want strange black blobs obscuring the peripheral vision. Those who wear spectacles should choose binoculars with fold-down rubber eye-cups. Most birdwatchers today prefer to use rubber-coated binoculars because they are easier to grip and are not as cold in winter.

the magical spectacle and sound of dozens of birds of different species swooping and chirping through woodland united by their common quest to eat.

One other reason that some birds form a flock is to keep warm. Birds need to maintain a very high body temperature of between 38 and 43 degrees Celsius. This is easier to do if they huddle together in a roost at night, or in the winter. Even wrens, antisocial, solitary little buggers ordinarily, will shack up in the cold winter months, with as many as three or four dozen clustered in a nest box to share body heat.

High fliers

The highest-flying bird ever recorded was a Ruppell's griffon vulture which collided with a commercial airliner, damaging one of the engines, over the Ivory Coast at 37,000 feet (11,250m) in 1973. In 1967, a wedge of whooper swans was seen at 27,000 feet (8,250m) by an airline pilot off the Scottish coast near the Hebrides. But bar-headed geese are probably the most frequent high fliers in the bird world. After breeding in Tibet they set off to spend the winter in the warmer climes of India, flying at over 18,000 feet (5,500m) to get through the Himalayas. A flock of these birds was once observed flying over the summit of Everest at least 30,000 feet (9,150m) above sea level.

MAKE YOUR OWN WINTER FEEDER IN MINUTES

Birds need food with a high energy content to keep them warm in the winter since their body reserves are quickly used up, particularly on very cold nights. You can help by making your own suet ball or bird cake, which is surprisingly quick and easy. Pour melted suet or lard on to a mixture of seeds, nuts, dried fruit, raw oatmeal, cheese and cake (two parts of these other foods to one part suet or lard). Stir well in a bowl and allow the goo to set in a container. An empty coconut shell or hard plastic cup makes a good feeder – or just turn the cake out on to the bird table.

Pole to Pole Without a Map

THE MYSTERY OF MIGRATION

The swallow is come!
The swallow is come!
O, fair are the seasons, and light
Are the days that she brings,
With her dusky wings,
And her bosom snowy white!

HENRY WADSWORTH LONGFELLOW

If birds have such small brains, how on earth do they know where to go when migrating thousands of miles?

How birds migrate is one of the great mysteries of nature. Some birds learn through following and observing their families, but others have no such guidance. The European cuckoo, for instance, is abandoned by its mother while still in the egg and left to be reared by a foster mother and yet, come the autumn, it takes wing for the African savannah as if it had been heading there all its life, which suggests that

its navigational information has been passed on genetically. The question has been baffling and amazing people for centuries, and there is no simple answer to it. In short, birds are known or are thought to use a whole range of navigational tools and techniques that vary from species to species.

- The **sun** is one of the most important navigational aids for many species. Birds have a form of internal clock by which they can calculate the exact time the sun takes to move through the sky, whatever the latitude and whatever the time of year. Even during cloudy and poor weather, birds can still work out the sun's position by the ultraviolet rays of polarized light that humans can't see. This back-up system is not perfect, though, and many birds get lost during prolonged cloudy weather.

- They will follow visual or **geographical landmarks** such as mountain ranges, coastlines and rivers.

- Like sailors of old, they use the **stars**; on cloudy nights, some birds lose their way.

- We know from scientific experiments that some birds use the **earth's magnetic field** to steer them to their destination. The birds fitted with little magnets to disrupt perception of the earth's magnetic field all got lost. Scientists found tiny particles of a magnetic mineral called magnetite in the head of some birds, leading them to believe they had an internal compass of some sort: the mineral can detect the earth's magnetic field, which gives the birds the ability to locate the position of magnetic north.

- Birds also orient themselves by detecting **infrasound**, a noise with a frequency so low humans can't hear it. The crash of wind and sea against land generates infrasound, which travels very long distances and helps migrant birds identify the landscape ahead.

- Some birds are born with a navigating **instinct** that has programmed them to head in a particular direction at certain times of year.

❝ Man feels himself an infinity above those creatures who stand, zoo-logically, only one step below him, but every human being looks up to the birds. They suit the fancy of us all. What they feel they can voice, as we try to; they court and nest, they battle with the elements, they are torn by two opposing impulses, a love of home and a passion for far places. Only with birds do we share so much emotion . . . birds seem to us like emissaries of another world which exists about us and above us, but into which, earthbound, we cannot penetrate. ❞

US WRITER DONALD CULROSS PEATTIE (1935)

Arctic tern: the long-distance champion

No other creature on earth sees as much sun as the tiny Arctic tern. In August, this remarkable seabird, not much bigger than a blackbird, leaves its breeding territories in the Arctic at the top of the planet and sets out on an epic journey to its winter quarters in the Antarctic at the bottom. It will follow one of three main routes: down western Europe and the West African coast; across the Atlantic and down the eastern seaboard of South America; or from northwest Canada down the west coast of the Americas. All three groups then cross the wild and stormy Great Southern Ocean. By the time it has returned to the Arctic, the tern will have flown an astonishing 25,000 miles. One of the reasons why it is able to achieve this feat is that, like many seabirds, it has adapted to feed and drink at sea, allowing it to refuel on the go.

(A growing shortage of fish stocks is starting to threaten some colonies.) One Arctic tern, ringed as a chick on the Farne Islands off the Northumberland coast, reached Melbourne in Australia just three months after it fledged.

Only the sooty shearwaters can rival the Arctic terns for long-distance migration. Every year, they set off on a remarkable circular journey that takes them from their breeding grounds in the Southern Ocean – including a large colony in the Falkland Islands – up the western side of the Pacific and Atlantic Oceans, to the coastlines near the Arctic Circle where they spend June and July. From there they head east, then south down the eastern side of the oceans to reach their nesting areas in November. Manx shearwaters, which breed in great numbers around the western coasts of the British Isles, are thought to make the same journey, but anticlockwise, heading down the Atlantic coast of South America to their winter quarters and then crossing the Atlantic to return via the African coast.

At the other end of the scale there are some species such as the wallcreeper and mountain quail that migrate no further than up and down the mountain or hill where they live.

Autumn Birds

The wild duck startles like a sudden thought,
And heron slow as if it might be caught.
The flopping crows on weary wings go by
And grey beard jackdaws noising as they fly.
The crowds of starnels whizz and hurry by,
And darken like a clod the evening sky.
The larks like thunder rise and suthy round,
Then drop and nestle in the stubble ground.
The wild swan hurries hight and noises loud
With white neck peering to the evening clowd.
The weary rooks to distant woods are gone.
With lengths of tail the magpie winnows on
To neighbouring tree, and leaves the distant crow
While small birds nestle in the edge below.

JOHN CLARE

Why do so many birds go to the incredible effort and risk of crossing half the planet twice a year?

It seems obvious that birds might want to leave Britain and northern Europe in the cold months of winter and go in search of food, but it's odd that they bother making the long and hazardous journey back every year from the warmth of Africa where food can be found all year round. It's exactly the same story across the Atlantic where billions make the twice-yearly epic odyssey between the continents of North and South America.

Leaving aside the question why they do it, even the basic facts of migration are a fairly recent discovery: the general understanding used to be that many birds hibernated. Highly intelligent, sensible people, including Dr Johnson, even believed that swallows spent the winter at the bottom of rivers.

Birds such as swallows and warblers, common sights in the UK in the warmer half of the year, are in fact African in origin and it's fairer to say that they visit us, rather than they winter in warmer climes before returning 'home'. They came north in the first place owing to the pressure of competition for food and mates.

During the last Ice Age much of northern and eastern Europe was covered in glaciers and ice sheets, and most birds and mammals lived in southern Europe and Africa. When the ice retreated towards the Arctic it left behind a lovely damp landscape rich in plants and buzzing with insects in the warmer months. Gradually, the birds and other animals headed north; some of them became permanent residents, but those birds that didn't like the cold started coming for the

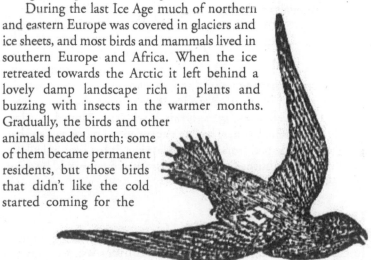

summer and returned south for the winter. Over millions of years these species redesigned themselves for the long journeys, growing longer wings, learning navigational skills and developing the ability to store fat to give them the necessary energy.

Summer in the more northerly latitudes provides not only an abundance of insects but also much longer days than you get in Africa, which means birds have more time to forage and feed their chicks in the breeding season. There are also fewer predators.

Migration is a dangerous enterprise and birds encounter many problems on the way and many of them will die, but, on balance, it makes evolutionary sense for them to shuttle thousands of miles back and forth each year.

Swallows certainly sleep all winter. A number of them conglobulate together, by flying round and round, and then all in a heap throw themselves under water, and lye in the bed of a river.

ENGLISH WRITER SAMUEL JOHNSON (1709–84)

700,000 miles to the gallon

The tiny blackpoll warbler, no larger than a blue tit, doubles its weight from about 11g to 21g to sustain it on its astonishing annual journey from Canada and the northeastern United States to South America. The non-stop flight, which is made by five billion warblers every autumn, covers between three and six thousand miles down the eastern seaboard of North America. By the time the bird arrives, about 90 hours after taking to the air, it will have flapped its wings roughly four million times, having expended no more energy than the amount to be had from a small Mars bar. It has been calculated that if the warbler burned up petrol rather than fat, it would be doing over 700,000 miles to the gallon.

That's just silly

For centuries it was believed that the barnacle goose hatched out of the barnacles growing on rocks along the British coast. Nor was this a conviction held only by the more dim-witted Britons in the Middle Ages – it wasn't until 1891, when the first nest was found in Greenland, that the myth was finally exploded. The study of migration had barely begun even then, and the old belief, which now seems so ludicrous, arose out of the fact these geese were never seen in the summer. That both the barnacles and the geese were black and white and a bit mottled, and they appeared in different seasons, apparently clinched it for our ancestors. If any Catholics knew the truth, they weren't going to let on. Barnacles being seafood, the goose which issued from a barnacle was counted as a fish and could therefore be eaten on Fridays and during Lent, when meat was forbidden by the Church.

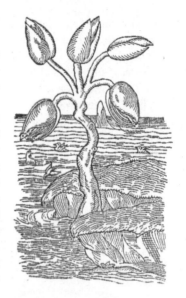

As to swallows being found in a torpid state during the winter in the Isle of Wight, or any part of this country, I never heard any such account worth attending to. But a clergyman, of an inquisitive turn, assures me that, when he was a great boy, some workmen, in pulling down the battlements of a church tower early in the spring, found two or three swifts among the rubbish, which were, at first appearance, dead, but, on being carried toward the fire, revived. He told me that, out of his great care to preserve them, he put them in a paper bag, and hung them by the kitchen fire, where they were suffocated.

Another intelligent person has informed me that, while he was a schoolboy at Brighthelmstone, in Sussex, a great fragment of the chalk cliff fell down one stormy winter on the beach; and that many people found swallows among the rubbish; but, on my questioning him whether he saw any of those birds himself, to my no small disappointment, he answered me in the negative; but that others assured him they did.

Young broods of swallows began to appear this year on July the eleventh, and young martins were then fledged in their nests. Both species will breed again once. For I see by my *Fauna* of last year, that young broods come forth so late as September the eighteenth. Are not these late hatchings more in favour of hiding than migration? Nay, some young martins remained in their nests last year so late as September the twenty-ninth; and yet they totally disappeared with us by the fifth of October.

How strange is it that the swift, which seems to live exactly the same life with the swallow and house-martin, should leave us before the middle of August invariably! while the latter stay often till the middle of October; and once I saw numbers of house-martins on the seventh of November. The martins and red-wing fieldfares were flying in sight together; an uncommon assemblage of summer and winter birds.

GILBERT WHITE, *NATURAL HISTORY AND ANTIQUITIES OF SELBORNE* (1789)

How do birds know when it's time to leave?

Hormonal changes and an intuitive or genetically inherited feel for the seasons tell birds when to up-nest and leave. Shorter days, a drop in air temperature and a decrease in local food supply are all signs telling the birds it's time to move on. But for many songbirds the

> *Migration study, complex though it is, still depends – and always will depend – on the observatory and field man, the island lover, the cape haunter and the sandwich eater.*
>
> JAMES FISHER, *SEA BIRDS*

trigger is a huge increase in appetite to fatten up for the long journey ahead. Timing its run is crucial to a bird's survival: go too early and there may not be enough food ready at the other end, but go too late and bad weather may claim it en route.

Birds are excellent weather forecasters and they wait for a period of high pressure with clear skies and favourable or light winds before setting out. Some of them can sense even the smallest change in barometric pressure and they will react to changes in the weather well before there is any visible sign of them.

Why do so many migrating birds always head straight for either Gibraltar or Istanbul?

Large, broad-winged birds, such as eagles, vultures, kites, buzzards and storks, rely on thermal columns of hot air in the atmosphere when they travel long distances. Thermals only occur over land, where heat from the sun-warmed earth rises high into the sky, to the delight of birds and hang-gliders alike. Soaring is a great way of saving energy as the bird barely needs to flap its wings. The wind all but carries it to its destination. These migratory species

Bird similes
Eat like a bird
Bald as a coot
Eyes like a hawk
Like a duck to water
Free as a bird
Like a headless chicken
Proud as a peacock
As wise as an owl
As graceful as a swan
As happy as a lark
Sing like a bird
Crazy as a loon
Like water off a duck's back
As the crow flies

A Manx shearwater, transported from its home in Wales and released in America, was back in its burrow on Skokholm Island off the Pembrokeshire coast 24 hours before the letter arrived announcing it had set off.

would find it impossible to cross large bodies of water as they cannot sustain active flight over more than short periods. Another consideration is that, whereas most migrating songbirds fatten up before setting out on their journey, birds of prey need to hunt along the way to maintain their energy levels.

The Mediterranean is therefore a major obstacle to soaring birds and so they have learned to cross it at its narrowest points. At peak migration times, massive numbers of birds of prey and storks pass through Gibraltar, Falsterbo and Istanbul. Gibraltar, that rocky outcrop of British territory, is wedged like a pebble in a crevice between Africa and Europe at the mouth of the Med. Falsterbo is the point where the southwest coast of Sweden comes close to the chain of Danish islands, allowing overland migrants to cross to mainland Europe in a series of short hops. Istanbul stands on the east side of the Bosphorus, a strait, just 640m at its narrowest, separating European from Asiatic Turkey and linking the Black Sea to the Mediterranean.

High mountain ranges present overland migrants with similar difficulties as great bodies of water, but the birds have learned to wend their way through a myriad passes and valleys to continue their vital journeys.

Eating on the go

Birds of prey and seabirds are not the only migratory birds that feed as they go. Swallows, swifts, martins and nightjars are just some species that eat insects en route. Sand martins forage for insects over water and their migratory routes run up and down the major rivers of Europe and Asia. In Britain they are found in greatest numbers over the larger rivers, such as the Trent and Severn, and once they reach Africa they follow the major waterways there, notably the Nile, which acts like a never-ending motorway and service station for the birds, laying out a clear route for them while offering a constant supply of provisions.

How do hundreds of millions of birds survive crossing the Sahara?

The Sahara desert is a vast stretch of baking sand and rock, the size of the United States and expanding by the year. Stretching from one side of northern Africa to the other, it is 1,000 miles wide north to south at its narrowest point, water sources are limited to a handful of oases, the daytime temperatures are blisteringly hot and at night it is perishingly cold. The Sahara is one of the most inhospitable regions of the planet but twice a year huge populations of little swallows, swifts, cuckoos, flycatchers and warblers somehow manage to cross it. How they achieve this remarkable feat of endurance is not yet understood. The birds emerge into the more temperate climes on either side of the desert exhausted, starving and dehydrated, but after a few days of voracious eating and drinking they are up and on their way once more. The journey stretches the birds to the limit and if it was much longer they would start to die en route – an alarming development which some scientists believe is already happening. The numbers of birds from sub-Saharan Africa that arrive in Britain for the summer have crashed in recent years and ornithologists believe that desertification of more

Random fate

Of six Brent geese fitted with £3,000 radio-tracking tags in Northern Ireland in May 2002, only one was known to have survived to the following winter, two fell victim to Arctic foxes and one, called Kerry, was found three months later in the freezer of an Inuit hunter on the remote Cornwallis Island off Canada.

swaths of previously fertile African land is one of the likely reasons behind the fall, along with the introduction of pesticides and new farming practices across the continent.

> Because the road is rough and long
> Shall we despise the skylark's song?
> **ENGLISH WRITER ANNE BRONTË (1820–49)**

Twice a year, migratory birds kept in captivity display a restlessness known by its German term *zugunruhe*, proving that in many species the migratory urge and the knowledge of when and in which direction to go are genetically inherited. At exactly the same time of year that their cousins in the wild are migrating to their other home, caged birds flap their wings and anxiously hop about on their perches. Many even point themselves in the direction in which they would be heading.

❝The years between the two great wars might be described as the years of reservoirs and sewage-farms, so far as British field ornithology is concerned. If anyone ever undertakes a serious research into the development of field studies among British birdwatchers, they may push the discovery of both reservoirs and sewage-farms further back . . . The attractiveness of the old-fashioned sewage-farm with its extensive muddy settling beds for migrating waders came later . . . The one generalisation that can now be made with assurance is that any good-sized pool or sewage-farm in any part of Midland England, whether near a river valley or not, will certainly attract plenty of birds of passage from time to time, waders, terns, gulls, ducks and others. Nor is this simply due to the fact that England is a small country with sea-coast a bare hundred miles away wherever you are. Watchers at such inland continental places as Geneva or Delhi have found that migrating seabirds turn up not infrequently, and not only after storms. ❞

H. G. ALEXANDER, *SEVENTY YEARS OF BIRDWATCHING*

WHEN TO SPOT MASS MIGRATIONS

Most migrating waders and songbirds travel at night and land to rest within an hour of sunrise. If you want to see these spectacular migrations, set your alarm for just before dawn. The birds travel under darkness because there is less chance of an attack by predators, they can forage for food during the day and the much cooler night-time temperatures reduce the risk of overheating or dehydration. Flying is easier too because typically the air is more stable than during the day when hotter air rises from the earth and the wind direction is more erratic. The night-fliers normally set out just before dusk in order to get their bearings from the setting sun and then plot their route according to the position of the moon and stars. Scientists have carried out experiments inside planetariums in which the birds behaved as if on a real migration.

No Nightingale did ever chaunt
More welcome notes to weary bands
Of travellers in some shady haunt,
Among Arabian sands:
A voice so thrilling ne'er was heard
In spring-time from the Cuckoo-bird,
Breaking the silence of the seas
Among the farthest Hebrides

WILLIAM WORDSWORTH

O Cuckoo! shall I call thee bird,
Or but a wandering voice?

WILLIAM WORDSWORTH

Swift numbers are declining because our buildings have become less welcoming to them. This spectacular summer visitor nests in roof spaces, finding gaps in eaves, tiles and brickwork of houses and outbuildings. A recent survey by the RSPB revealed that the swift shows a marked preference for buildings built before the First World War, presumably because there are more points of entry in the ageing structures. As our old buildings are renovated or torn down and replaced with new ones, the swift's housing options are slowly disappearing.

> True hope is swift, and flies with swallow's wings;
> Kings it makes gods, and meaner creatures kings.
> **WILLIAM SHAKESPEARE (1564–1616)**

HOW TO SAFEGUARD SWIFT HOMES

- Wherever possible, leave existing nest holes alone.
- If it's necessary to remove the nest and fill up the hole, fit an internal nest box and make a hole at the same location as the original nest site.
- Create new sites by making appropriately sized holes in buildings swifts are known to frequent.
- Fit internal nest boxes in new builds or extensions.
- Use external, wall-mounted nest boxes as a last resort.

> See! from the brake the whirring pheasant springs,
> And mounts exulting on triumphant wings:
> Short is his joy; he feels the fiery wound,
> Flutters in blood, and panting beats the ground.
> **ENGLISH POET ALEXANDER POPE (1688–1744)**

Slaughter in the Med

In recent years, conservation groups have been turning up the political heat on the governments of southern Europe to bring an end to the annual slaughter of millions of birds, including many increasingly rare species such as the lesser kestrel, osprey and purple heron. Hunters in Malta, Cyprus, Italy, Portugal and parts of France are seen as the worst offenders, wiping out the birds in the migration season in the name of sport. In days gone by, the hunters killed for food; today they do it for fun, taxidermy and target practice. Malta alone has nearly 12,000 hunters and over 4,500 trappers in a population of just 400,000. As a direct result of the persecution, only 21 species of bird breed in Malta today.

Many of the birds are protected by law but it is difficult to stop the hunters due to a

Many migrant birds that are not usually gregarious will flock together before and/or during migration for the same reasons that social or colony birds do it all the time. As a team, they have more chance of seeking out food sources and finding the way to their destination, and each individual has less chance of being taken by a predator.

lack of political will, opposition from the hunters and trappers and a shortage of law enforcement officers on the ground. The RSPB and other conservation organizations in the north of Europe argue that it is their business to get involved because many of the species being killed are our summer visitors making their way to or from their winter homes. Live-trapping is also widely practised so the hunters can use the birds as caged pets or as decoys. Trapping methods include sticks covered in glue which fixes the bird when it lands on them, nets, snares and lures – such as live decoys, food bait or sound-recordings of bird song.

Bird wrecks

Although many birds are able to forecast weather in the short term, there is little they can do if they are hit by a storm midway through their migratory journey. The strong winds may blow seabirds hundreds, even thousands of miles off course in an event known as a 'bird wreck'. Many will never complete their journey, dying of exhaustion in their struggle to get back on course. Others will be blown off their usual routes over the open seas and on to land where they will settle for a few days' rest and wait for the storm to pass before trying to reorient themselves. These can be exciting moments for bird-watchers as they flock to see

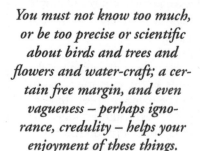

You must not know too much, or be too precise or scientific about birds and trees and flowers and water-craft; a certain free margin, and even vagueness – perhaps ignorance, credulity – helps your enjoyment of these things.

WALT WHITMAN

unfamiliar visitors to their shores. Ringing evidence has shown that, from time to time, some species from the Americas, blown over to Britain in a period of extreme weather, have chosen to join their foreign cousins on the winter migration to Africa and have returned across the Atlantic the following spring. A 'wreck' is distinct from a 'fall' in which migrating birds, usually songbirds, are forced to descend on to the land below and wait for a break in the bad weather before continuing their journey.

Robin Redbreast

Good-bye, good-bye to Summer!
  For Summer's nearly done;
The garden smiling faintly,
  Cool breezes in the sun;
Our Thrushes now are silent,
  Our Swallows flown away, –
But Robin's here, in coat of brown,
  With ruddy breast-knot gay.
    Robin, Robin Redbreast,
      O Robin dear!
    Robin sings so sweetly
      In the falling of the year.

Bright yellow, red, and orange,
  The leaves come down in hosts;
The trees are Indian Princes,
  But soon they'll turn to Ghosts;
The scanty pears and apples
  Hang russet on the bough;
It's Autumn, Autumn, Autumn late,
  'Twill soon be Winter now.
    Robin, Robin Redbreast,
      O Robin dear!
    And welaway! my Robin,
      For pinching days are near.

The fire-side for the cricket,
  The wheatstack for the mouse,
When trembling night-winds whistle
  And moan all round the house.
The frosty ways like iron,
  The branches plumed with snow, –
Alas! in winter dead and dark,
  Where can poor Robin go?
    Robin, Robin Redbreast,
      O Robin dear!
    And a crumb of bread for Robin,
      His little heart to cheer!

IRISH POET WILLIAM ALLINGHAM (1824–89)

Just Behave

THE REMARKABLE BEHAVIOUR OF BIRDS

Why are robins so friendly ... or are they?

The robin, Britain's favourite bird, is a cute little chap who sits on your spade, sings you a song and makes you feel like St Francis of Assisi. It's just a hop or two away from sitting on your shoulder and, if you had the patience to stand around in your vegetable patch like a scarecrow for a week, it would even eat out of your hand. The robin likes you because, well, without being big-headed or anything, you've just got a way with animals . . .

Er, wrong, human fool. You have been flattered and duped by a creature with a brain the size of a Smartie. That adorable little red-breasted crooner is, in fact, a nasty, aggressive little bugger, who's only after your worms and would happily peck out his mother's eyes to defend his dinner. You are but a means to an end, an imbecile in a multi-pocketed gardening apron, turning over the soil for Mr Chirpy-Chirpy Redbreast to dine out on some nice juicy earthworms.

All birds are territorial in the sense that they need a plot of land, or stretch of water, where they can live, breed and feed. But the robin is more territorial than most, one of a handful of birds that hold a territory all year round. In spring and summer, during the breeding season, the mating pair defend their land aggressively, but in the winter each bird will find and protect its own patch with the same ferocity. Control over a good plot, rich in food sources, is the only way to survive. For the robin, as for the estate agent, the maxim is 'Location! Location! Location!' Without a good plot of land or the ability to defend it, beak and claw, the robin will quickly die of starvation. Hence the fierce determination to stand its ground against intruders and rivals.

In areas where food supplies are at a premium or where the robin population has boomed after a good breeding season, fights are common and often end in death. The mere sight of a red patch on an object roughly resembling a robin will often prompt an attack. So if you find yourself at a loose end one day – and I mean very loose – make a stuffed robin from an old sock, complete with red patch, and place it in the middle of your garden, then sit back and wait for the real one to swoop in and attack it. Hilarious. Who's the thicko now, Mr Chirpy-Chirpy Redbreast, eh?

The Truth
Since I have seen a bird one day,
His head pecked more than half away;
That hopped about, with but one eye,
Ready to fight again, and die –
Ofttimes since then their private lives
Have spoilt that joy their music gives.

So when I see this robin now,
Like a red apple on the bough,
And question why he sings so strong,
For love, or for the love of song;
Or sings, maybe, for that sweet rill
Whose silver tongue is never still –

Ah, now there comes this thought unkind,
Born of the knowledge in my mind:
He sings in triumph that last night
He killed his father in a fight;
And now he'll take his mother's blood –
The last strong rival for his food.

W. H. DAVIES

Never trust a bird with a beard

The bearded tit is an odd little bird, and its habits, evolutionary history and flight are just as quirky as its appearance and as amusing as its name. For a start, it's not really a tit. It belongs to a family of birds called parrotbills that live in Asia. Secondly, it doesn't have a beard. The plump little reedbed-dweller with the jaunty undulating flight is not closely related to any other European species, and it has what people whose job it is to describe the appearance of birds call a 'moustache', in the form of a black stripe running down each side of its face from the eye, like non-waterproof mascara.

The bearded tit even eats oddly. In the breeding season it eats insects, and can be seen shimmying up and down reed stems (if you're lucky, that is, because it's a shy creature). When the seeds start to fall to the ground, it scratches around in the dirt, just like a chicken. The switch from eating soft juicy insects to hard seeds forces the walls of its digestive system to develop incredibly strong muscle tissue. To help grind down and mince up the hard-shelled seeds, the bearded tit will swallow up to 400 tiny pieces of grit, giving it a bloated appearance in the winter. They have always been vulnerable to severe winters, but their numbers have declined sharply in recent years despite the milder climate.

Hedgerow hooligans

No one likes magpies but, like Millwall football fans, they don't care. They just keep rampaging through the nation's hedgerows killing nestlings and stealing eggs in their millions. The gamekeepers who used to keep their numbers in check have disappeared from the countryside faster than cuckoos and nightingales. In the absence of proper research showing the impact of magpies on other bird numbers, conservation bodies are reluctant to back action against this noisy crow.

The sheer number of magpies is a part of the problem. Since 1970 they have increased by 96 per cent and spread into new territories. The car must shoulder a great deal of the blame. With more and more carrion littering our roads, magpies and other scavengers are enjoying a year-round ready-made meal where previously their numbers were probably kept down by a lack of food in the winter.

The Dying Swan

The plain was grassy, wild and bare,
Wide, wild, and open to the air,
Which had built up everywhere
  An under-roof of doleful gray.
With an inner voice the river ran,
Adown it floated a dying swan,
    And loudly did lament.
  It was the middle of the day.
Ever the weary wind went on,
    And took the reed-tops as it went.

Some blue peaks in the distance rose,
And white against the cold-white sky,
Shone out their crowning snows.
  One willow over the river wept,
And shook the wave as the wind did sigh;
Above in the wind was the swallow,
  Chasing itself at its own wild will,
  And far thro' the marish green and still
  The tangled water-courses slept,
Shot over with purple, and green, and yellow.

The wild swan's death-hymn took the soul
Of that waste place with joy
Hidden in sorrow: at first to the ear
The warble was low, and full and clear;

And floating about the under-sky,
Prevailing in weakness, the coronach stole
Sometimes afar, and sometimes anear;
But anon her awful jubilant voice,
With a music strange and manifold,
Flow'd forth on a carol free and bold;
As when a mighty people rejoice
With shawms, and with cymbals, and harps of gold,
And the tumult of their acclaim is roll'd
Thro' the open gates of the city afar,
To the shepherd who watcheth the evening star.
And the creeping mosses and clambering weeds,
And the willow-branches hoar and dank,
And the wavy swell of the soughing reeds,
And the wave-worn horns of the echoing bank,
And the silvery marish-flowers that throng
The desolate creeks and pools among,
Were flooded over with eddying song.

ENGLISH POET ALFRED, LORD TENNYSON (1809–92)

A squadron of Shitfires

The fieldfare, a thrush that flies from Scandinavia to spend the winter in Britain, has a unique way of repelling predators: it shits on them. From a great height, needless to say. If a crow, magpie, jay or bird of prey tries to raid their loosely spread colonies in the woods during the breeding season, the fieldfares scramble to the skies like a squadron of Spitfires, their siren squawks filling the air, and proceed to launch a series of dive-bombing sorties, each time unloading a squirt of shit on the intruders. Sometimes they will even ram into them. The attack is more than just an unpleasant inconvenience for the predator – it can be fatal, albeit in rare cases. The uric acid in the shit has a corrosive effect on plumage, and without its feathers a bird is as good as dead. British predators need have no fears, however, because the attacks normally only take place during the breeding season in Scandinavia, although occasionally fieldfares will deploy the same 'bombing' tactics to defend a favourite feeding ground.

The fieldfare is also one of the earliest risers in the avian community, appearing up to 90 minutes before dawn, according to the people whose job it is to get up in the middle of the night to check these things.

The highwayman of the high seas

Skuas (Arctic skuas and great skuas) are the scourge of sea-cliff colonies, built to mug, rob and kill. With its powerful beak and clawed webs, the skua worked out fairly early in its evolution that life would be far easier if it let other seabirds do the often exhausting job of finding the fish. The skua saves its energy by waiting back near land for a gannet or tern or puffin to return with a mouth full of goodies. It then intercepts and robs the hunter at beak point. Both species of skua eat chicks but the great skua will also eat a small bird such as the puffin. You too might be reluctant, at the end of a 200-mile round shopping trip to feed your young, to hand over your provisions to a violent intruder waiting on your doorstep. Though some manage to fly their way out of trouble, most birds are no match for a skua if it comes down to a straight one-on-one scrap. The exception is the gannet, which is larger than a skua and will give as good as it gets, aided by its long sharp beak that has been adapted for skewering fish when it plunges into the sea from 100 feet.

It's a relief perhaps that these aerial hooligans are only summer visitors to the very north of Scotland and its outlying islands, although they pass through all coastal areas of Britain. If you see a skua overhead, there's only one thing to do: hide your puffins.

Who you calling common?

The common gull is not in fact as common as the black-headed gull and the herring gull, familiar sights on the nation's rubbish tips and recreation grounds. The screeching scavenger that eats virtually anything and robs other birds of their food may not be the most popular bird in town, but it does perform a charming dance routine. When it's particularly wet underfoot, look out for the gulls, running on the spot on playing fields and other stretches of open grass. The stomping is thought to mimic the drumming of rain and forces the worms to come to the surface to avoid drowning in the soupy morass created by the boogying bird.

> A mute swan is so called because, unlike the whooper and Bewick's swans, it doesn't call while flying.

Why do some birds like to bathe in the dust at the side of roads?

'Dusting' is common among birds living in arid climates, but some birds in a temperate climate like ours, such as larks, sparrows and wrens, will also wash in dust if there's no water to be found. Dusting is part of a bird's rigorous preening regime. Most birds store oil in a

Bird sayings
A bird in the hand is worth two in the bush.
Birds of a feather flock together.
The early bird catches the worm.
To kill two birds with one stone.
You're counting your chickens before they've hatched.
The chickens have come home to roost.

gland under their tail, and they rub it over their plumage with their beaks. When they want to clean the feathers on their head, they wipe the oil on their feet and then smear it on their heads. The oil has antibacterial, fungicidal and waterproofing qualities. Scientists believe that dusting helps birds rid the feathers of parasites, debris and excess oil.

Why do birds sunbathe?

Some birds, notably blackbirds but also others including pigeons, thrushes, robins and sparrows, can occasionally be seen sunbathing, lying face down on a warm, safe spot such as a roof, with wings and tail feathers outstretched. Quite why they do this is not fully understood but the experts suspect it is related to the maintenance of their plumage. There are four theories: 1) the sun's rays help the spread of preening oil through the feathers; 2) parasites are lured to the surface where the bird can pick them off more easily; 3) the ultraviolet light converts chemicals in the preening oil into vitamin D; 4) it may simply be that the birds are using the sun to help them save energy, by boosting the high body temperature they need to maintain.

There was an Old Man with a beard,
Who said, 'It is just as I feared! –
    Two Owls and a Hen,
    Four Larks and a Wren,
Have all built their nests in my beard!'
ENGLISH WRITER EDWARD LEAR (1812–88)

Why do some birds rub themselves with ants?

Over 200 species of birds indulge in the weird activity of 'anting', spreading themselves over an anthill or nest and letting the insects run amok in their feathers. Some birds pick up the ants in their beaks and rub them over their feathers. Either way, the birds often seem to reach a point of ecstasy while they are anting. Blackbirds, starlings and jays are Britain's most enthusiastic anters. Experts believe the formic acid released by the ants may help kill off lice and other parasites, but as with so much bird behaviour, it's still a mystery.

Birds who do what their names suggest
Turnstone
Woodpecker
Treecreeper
Dipper
Nuthatch
Flycatcher
Wagtail
Shoveler

Be very wary of the cassowary

The third largest flightless bird after the ostrich and the emu, the cassowary is a shy creature living deep in the forests of northern Australia and Papua New Guinea, but if provoked or cornered it will lash out with its powerful legs and claws. Regarded as the most fearsome bird on the planet, it has been known to disembowel a man with a single kick.

Why do some birds like to spread their wings over a smoking chimney pot?

Birds such as rooks and starlings can sometimes be seen perching over smoking chimneys with their wings fully extended, and some have even been seen to rub themselves with a smoking cigarette butt. On rare occasions both houses and treetops have been set on fire when a bird has taken a burning butt back to its nest. Just as they are still baffled by the mysteries of anting and sunbathing, scientists have yet to crack the puzzle of why some birds like to 'smoke-bathe', but as with the other two bizarre activities, it is probably to do with grooming and ridding themselves of irritating parasites.

Why do seabirds, often millions of them, form giant cities on cliffs and rocks?

In spite of drawing the attention of predators by the incredible noise and commotion, not to mention the hideous stink of their guano, seabirds are safer living in great numbers and have a better chance of breeding successfully than if they split up into pairs. Even the most ferocious predator will turn tail under attack from a thousand screeching gannets or gulls. The birds are also playing a percentage game, knowing that the greater their number, the smaller the chance they have of falling victim to a raid. The same principle applies to crime on a crowded Underground train – there are only so many pockets a pickpocket can rifle, so the busier it is the less likely it is that any individual passenger will be robbed. What's more, as any teenager at a disco will testify, a crowded dance floor is a better place to find a date than a phone booth. The noise and excitement of a sea colony stimulates the ovaries and testes of the birds. The third advantage of living in a giant community is that the birds are able to pool their resources to help locate passing shoals of fish.

The waters around the British Isles boast some of the most important bird breeding colonies on the planet but it should be noted that not all birds enjoy living in these cliff-face cities as it means sharing their living quarters with some extremely ill-mannered neighbours such as fulmars and great black-backed gulls, truly the ASBO families of the avian world.

The truth is that these birds have little choice because there just aren't enough cliffs to go round.

Why do parrots lick clay?

Wild parrots, parakeets and macaws eat a lot of nuts and seeds that contain poisonous chemicals and it is thought that they lick and gnaw clay to help absorb the toxins. Along the banks of the Amazonian river network are many stretches of clay deposits known as 'licks' where the colourful birds congregate in their hundreds. Clay is rich in alkaline minerals, including calcium compounds, which help counteract stomach acid and aid digestion.

Why do owls and other birds of prey get 'mobbed' by dozens of other birds?

In a nutshell, 'small bird syndrome', a phenomenon of animal behaviour similar to 'short man syndrome', aka the Napoleon Complex, in which the male of the species *Homo sapiens* lashes out at his bigger rivals in order to prove that his physical shortcomings are no bar to virility, generally after feeding too well on strong continental lager. In the avian world, the smaller creatures have more pressing and forgivable reasons for taking on the local bully. They do this as a group, swirling around the predator in a mad, squawking, screeching frenzy and driving it out of the immediate vicinity. Differences between species are set aside as all manner of small birds including blackbirds, robins, finches and tits join forces to see off an intruder. Most mobbing takes place in the breeding season, especially once the chicks have hatched and are starting to fledge. Owls and other birds of prey, magpies, crows and jays often find themselves on the receiving end of a mobbing, but other animals including cats, foxes and even humans also get attacked. Gulls, terns and crows are amongst the most ferocious and alarming of mobbers.

Nice family

The fulmar's name means 'foul gull' and comes from its habit of spewing dark smelly gunk over unwelcome visitors. Just as a fieldfare will shit on a predator to drive it away, the fulmar, a summer visitor to Britain, will spit out oily gunge from its stomach with the accuracy of a champion darts player. The disgusting substance has the same corrosive effect on a bird's plumage as a fieldfare's flying turd. The chicks of the fulmar, a relation of the altogether better-mannered albatross, can do their own gobbing after just 14 days.

> The plural of goose is geese,
> But the plural of moose ain't meese,
> And the plural of noose ain't neese,
> But the plural of goose – is geese.
> **ROLAND YOUNG (1887–1953)**

Screech for the sky

In 1621, a famous aerial battle took place between two huge flocks of starlings over the city of Cork in southern Ireland. It lasted for three days and led to the deaths of thousands of birds, whose mutilated bodies fell into the streets and fields to the astonishment of the people watching below. A man called Nicholas Bourne collected testimonies from witnesses to the battle, which darkened the sky and filled the air with demonic screeching between 12 and 14 October. He published a pamphlet entitled _The Wonderfull Battell of Starelings_.

One flock of starlings had gathered in the east and one in the west of the city, bringing the two into conflict over the territory they each wanted to claim for food and roosting. The battle began with a series of skirmishes and what appeared to onlookers to be a series of reconnaissance missions by small squadrons of birds from each camp. After a few days, the main fighting erupted when both flocks took to the skies and flew straight at each other. Bourne describes what happened: 'Upon a strange sound and noise made as well on the one side as on the other, they

THE
WONDERFVLL
Battell of Starelings:

Fought at the Citie of *Corke* in *Ireland*, the 12. and 14. of October laft paft. 1621.

As it hath bin incredibly enformed by diuers Noble-men, and others of the faid Kingdome, &c.

LONDON,
Printed for N. B. 1622.

forthwith at one instant took wing, and so mounting up into the skies, encountered one another with such a terrible shock, as the sound amazed the whole citie . . . Upon this sudden and fierce encounter, there fell down into the citie, and into the rivers, multitudes of starelings, some with wings broken, some with legs and necks broken, some with eyes picked out, some their bills thrust into the breasts and sides of their adversaries.'

The battle raged until dusk and the following day it erupted again, this time 400 miles away over the Thames estuary in London. Passengers on the Woolwich ferryboat reported seeing 'infinite multitudes of starlings fighting in all violent manner together, with a crow or raven flying betwixt them'. The following morning the birds were back over Cork where 'More dead birds rained down upon the streets and houses, but this time among them were found the mangled bodies of a kite, a raven, and a crow.' The fighting continued into the afternoon until, in an instant, both flocks, now considerably smaller and worn out by their exertions, disappeared in different directions.

Eight months later the city was ravaged by fire after a series of lightning strikes in a storm. The feeling amongst the locals was that the two incidents were linked and that they were being punished for their wickedness. A long ballad called 'The Lamentable Burning of the City of Corke' by an unknown author was published not long afterwards.

Do birds that attack windows have mental health problems?

If you have ever seen a drunk fighting his own reflection in a shop window, then you will have some idea of what our garden birds are doing when they swoop up to the kitchen window and start pecking at it furiously. It can be quite an alarming spectacle, with the bird seemingly trying to get into the house – as if an extra from Hitchcock's *The Birds* has escaped from the film set and come to peck out our eyes. But in fact it is simply a case of mistaken identity. Very mistaken. The bird thinks it's attacking a rival, but is in fact actually hammering away at its own reflected image. You may find that funny, but the truth is that when birds began to evolve tens of millions of years ago, there were no windows around for them to absorb into their experience and adapt accordingly. We, the window inventors, are to blame for their folly. This behaviour is territorial and occurs during the breeding season when male birds, testosterone coursing through their bodies, stake out their patch of garden, attract a mate and then defend her from intruders and interlopers. A great many garden birds attack their own reflection at this time of year wherever they come across it in or close to the territory they are defending. As well as windows, they will also launch themselves at car wing mirrors, shiny hub caps and bumpers and even sun roofs. Although the bird will lose valuable energy fighting its own image, it comes to no harm and will eventually return to the important tasks of building the family nest, copulating with its partner and rearing its young.

HOW TO AVOID WINDOW FATALITIES

Windows cause the deaths of millions of birds every year, and the cleaner the window, the greater the threat they pose. On bright days, the glass reflects the world beyond and birds are fooled into flying straight at them. Big, tall French windows are the serial killers of the glass world. Many birds break their necks on collision and die, although some are simply stunned and manage to come round before they wake up in the mouth of the resident cat. One simple solution is to put a few stickers on the glass on the outside of the window. Images of birds, especially birds of prey, have proved to be a very effective deterrent.

Walking underwater

The dipper, a plump little bird with a white bib, walks along the bed of fast-flowing streams and small rivers turning over stones in search of food. It is the only bird that can do this. It stops itself floating to the surface by digging its toes into the bed of the stream. Its stubby wings are well adapted for swimming and it has its own built-in goggles that are activated underwater, as well as a large preening gland for oiling and waterproofing its feathers.

Why do we see so few dead birds?

Although tens of millions of birds die every year in the UK, it is very rare to come across a dead body, save for a pheasant in the road or a pigeon that has been ambushed by a sparrowhawk. A crucial link in the food chain, most small birds are eaten by mammals and other birds, explaining why many species produce so many offspring. Once they have finished with the flesh of the bird, scavengers and predators such as foxes, cats and rats will leave only the feathers behind and these will soon be scattered by the winds or swallowed up by the undergrowth. Sick birds, like many animals, retreat into secluded hideaways to recover and are unlikely to be found if they die there. A bird that does just drop dead will decompose very quickly as the insects get to work on its light body mass.

Lock up your goats

The nightjar, a highly camouflaged nocturnal bird with a sinister reputation, has been making a strong comeback in recent years after decades of decline. The destruction of 45 per cent of southern England's heathland, the bird's natural habitat, since the 1950s has taken its toll on this summer visitor to Britain from tropical Africa, but thanks to the efforts of conservation groups its numbers are up to roughly 4,500 pairs from about 3,000 just 15 years ago. This dove-sized bird that looks like a cross between a kestrel and a cuckoo nests on the ground but feeds on the wing, following animal flocks and herds to snaffle moths and other insects that appear amongst them at dusk. Its distinctive 'churring' call has led to it being given a number of alternative names including 'gabble ratchet' (Yorkshire) and 'scissors grinder' (Norfolk). For centuries, the nightjar was scorned by country folk who, hearing but rarely seeing this weird-sounding creature amongst their livestock, came to believe it was stealing the milk from the animals. Thus it came to be widely known as 'the goatsucker' and even its official Latin name, *Caprimulgus*, means exactly that.

> *You cannot prevent the birds of sorrow from flying over your head, but you can prevent them from building nests in your hair.*
>
> CHINESE PROVERB

Voles are just pissing into the wind

When you see a kestrel hovering at the side of a road or field, it is looking for its favourite food, the vole. How these birds of prey, up to 20 metres above the ground, manage to see the tiny rodents shuffling nervously beneath the undergrowth had never been satisfactorily explained – until recently. Yes, kestrels like all birds of prey have tremendous eyesight, but the suspicion was that there was more to it than that. Voles are seriously small and they spend most of their time under the cover of vegetation, only rarely emerging into the open. From time to time, vole populations suffer sudden and huge crashes, forcing kestrels to travel hundreds of miles to find new vole-rich territory. How do they find these new areas so quickly, before they die of starvation? In 1995, Finnish scientists at the University of Turku produced the surprising explanation: the birds can see the trail of urine that voles leave wherever they go. Voles widdle as they go, because they use the urine as a navigation aid and as a way of communicating with each other. The trails are visible in ultraviolet light, which kestrels can detect, a skill which enables them to scan large areas in a short time.

The Tyson of the treetops

The hawfinch is Britain's largest finch and possibly our most elusive bird. Shy and jumpy, it takes wing at the drop of a hazelnut in a neighbouring county. It's also awful at singing and so, even if it let us get within viewing distance, we'd be unaware of its presence. What's more, it lives right in the top of tree canopies, so you can't see it anyway. In fact, perhaps the hawfinch doesn't even exist and is nothing more than an ornithologist's April Fool hoax that has been running for years. Those who claim to have seen one say it has a head and neck like Mike Tyson and an astonishingly powerful beak that can wield a force of more than 50kg – almost 1,000 times its body weight – and is capable of cracking a cherry stone in five seconds.

Why does the robin eat alone and the sparrow in a group?

The house sparrow lives off seeds and scraps which are often found in patches, and it is a more efficient use of energy if a cluster of the birds seek out these food sources. The birds work as a team and when one strikes it lucky, the others arrive to join in the bonanza before they all move on in search of more. This group foraging is also common among many seabirds seeking shoals of fish. Its virtue is that between them the birds form a mobile information centre, with each bird supplying and responding to the pooled information. Like the blackbird and the thrush, the robin is a solitary feeder owing to the fact that it eats mainly worms and insects from the ground. The last thing it wants to do when it plucks a nice fat earthworm from the soil is invite the neighbours round to share its catch.

Bird Brain

INSTINCT OR INTELLIGENCE?

How intelligent are birds?

A bird can't read a book or work out compound interest rates, but then again a man can't navigate his way from South Africa to the same nest site in Northamptonshire every spring. If you lay the dissected brains of a human being and a bird alongside each other, a man in a long white coat (with a brain the size of Kettering) will be able to point out why the intelligence of the two creatures is so different. The most highly developed part of man's brain is the cerebral cortex, the area for learning and remembering, explaining why man can write piano concertos and work out the theory of relativity. The most highly developed area in a bird is the cerebellum, which controls movement and coordination, explaining why a bird can weave in and out of a thousand branches at 30mph in fading light without crashing.

> *Those little nimble musicians of the air that warble forth their curious ditties with which nature hath furnished them to the shame of art.*
>
> ENGLISH WRITER IZAAK WALTON (1593–1683)

The front part of the bird brain is smaller than a mammal's and the most important section of it is the diencephalon where genetically inherited information is retained. It is this area of the brain which informs, say, a young cuckoo, setting out by itself on its first migration, exactly where to go. Most birds fly the family nest as soon as they can fly, a matter of weeks in most species, whereas human young stay and learn from their parents for a very long period before making their own way in the world. Social birds, such as blue tits, will imitate their parents to a certain extent, but mostly they rely upon a combination of instinct, prompted by the genetic computer in their forebrain, and trial and error. If they eat a berry or an insect that makes them sick, they will know not to eat it again.

The learning capacity of birds is very limited – though crows and parrots, the most 'intelligent' birds by human standards, might buttonhole you about that. They are among a handful of birds that can learn new tricks. Crows in Japanese cities drop walnuts in front of cars at traffic lights then sit on the overhead pylons and wait for an obliging wheel to break the shell open. A crow can also strip a stick of leaves and off-shoots and use it as a tool for digging out grubs. The song thrush works out that it can get at the flesh of a snail by

> *I never saw a wild thing sorry for itself. A small bird will drop frozen dead from a bough without ever having felt sorry for itself.*
>
> ENGLISH WRITER D. H. LAWRENCE (1885–1930)

dashing its shell against a rock. Sparrows are consistently inventive in their search for food, raiding spiders' webs for insects and even the grilles of cars where insects collect.

Birds have very little consciousness: they don't reflect on the past, or project their thoughts into the future. They live in the now and are only interested in knowledge that helps them to survive. It may take tens of thousands of years for that information to sink in. But that doesn't make birds stupid. If they were stupid, they'd go and talk to a cat. Or start wars and put all their money in the stock exchange.

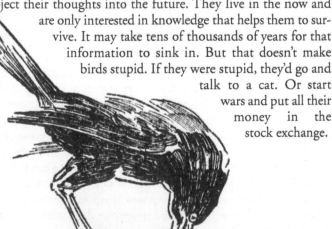

The Kingfisher

It was the Rainbow gave thee birth,
  And left thee all her lovely hues;
And, as her mother's name was Tears,
  So runs it in thy blood to choose
For haunts the lonely pools, and keep
In company with trees that weep.

Go you and, with such glorious hues,
  Live with proud Peacocks in green parks;
On lawns as smooth as shining glass,
  Let every feather show its marks;
Get thee on boughs and clap thy wings
Before the windows of proud kings.

Nay, lovely Bird, thou art not vain;
  Thou hast no proud ambitious mind;
I also love a quiet place
  That's green, away from all mankind;
A lonely pool, and let a tree
Sigh with her bosom over me.

W. H. DAVIES

How and why does a starling mimic the ring of my mobile phone?

An African grey parrot called Alex achieved minor celebrity for having built up a vocabulary of 800 words during his long life but it's not just fancy captive birds that can learn the sounds created by human beings and their machines. A number of wild birds are equally adept at mimicry, including the lyrebirds and bower-birds of Australasia and the mockingbirds of the Americas. Even the humble blackbird and starling hopping about in your garden can put Alistair McGowan or Rory Bremner to shame with the accuracy of their sound representation. If you exposed them to the whining sound long enough, all these birds could imitate an Australian international sportsman to perfection.

You may well have heard the ring of a mobile phone, the wail of an ambulance siren, the jaunty tune of a man whistling or the unmistakable high-pitched, block-nosed warble of a David Beckham and not realized that it was in fact a small bird sitting on a nearby roof running through its latest repertoire. Not, by any means, that all blackbirds and starlings spend their days running through a catalogue of impressions, but if they hear certain sounds for long enough, then eventually they will start to repeat them.

Songbirds learn their songs from the adults around them, mainly from the males, who do far more vocalizing than the females. If a bird is constantly exposed to the song of a different species then it will learn its neighbour's repertoire too. And if that bird happens to live next to a house or office where it can hear the constant trill of a tele-

phone, then eventually it will learn to imitate that sound as well. Ornithologists suspect that birds mimic sounds for the same reason that they sing their lungs out in spring: to make themselves more attractive to a female and to intimidate any rivals at the start of the breeding season. There's nothing a female bird likes more than to be serenaded by a desperate male banging out the sound of a police siren or a pneumatic drill from the treetops.

The common cormorant or shag
Lays eggs inside a paper bag
The reason you will see no doubt
It is to keep the lightning out
But what these unobservant birds
Have never noticed is that herds
Of wandering bears may come with buns
And steal the bags to hold the crumbs.

ENGLISH NOVELIST CHRISTOPHER ISHERWOOD (1904–86)

Mozart-whistling starling

The great Austrian composer Mozart bought a starling from a pet store in 1784 after hearing it whistle the beginning of the last movement of his Piano Concerto No.17 in G major, K453. Although the silly bird sang G sharp instead of G natural, Mozart was still mightily impressed and took him home, jotting the date, price and the notes the bird was singing into an expenses book. When the bird died, three years later, Mozart buried it in his garden and recited a poem he wrote to mark the solemn occasion.

A bird does not sing because it has an answer. It sings because it has a song.

CHINESE PROVERB

I'd teach a starling how to speak and sing,
Till every word and note with truth should ring,
With all the skill my lips and tongue impart,
With all the warmth and passion of my heart.
Then let him brightly sing it through her windowpane:
Thine is my heart, Thine is my heart,
And shall forever, forever so remain!

GERMAN POET WILHELM MÜLLER (1794–1827), FROM *DIE SCHÖNE MÜLLERIN*
(THE BEAUTIFUL MILL GIRL), A POEM TURNED INTO A WELL-KNOWN SONG
CYCLE BY AUSTRIAN COMPOSER FRANZ SCHUBERT

Collective nouns of some common birds

A murder of crows
A kettle of hawks
A charm of hummingbirds
An exaltation of larks
A parliament of
    owls/rooks
A bevy of quail
An unkindness of ravens

A wisp of snipe
A chatter of starlings
A pitying of turtledoves
A knob of widgeons
A plump of wildfowl
A fall of woodcocks
A herd of wrens

Hollywood crows

Alfred Hitchcock used over 600 real birds alongside a number of stuffed and mechanical ones in the filming of his classic 1963 horror film *The Birds*. Crows, seagulls, hawks, ravens, eagles, finches and starlings were trained for several months to become feathered actors, to add some terrifying realism to the scenes. The crows were the stars of the show, according to trainer Ray Berwick who taught his favourite one, Nosey, to fetch his car keys and even to put a cigarette in his mouth and light it for him. 'I'm amazed at the reasoning power of the crow,' Berwick told *Time* magazine during filming in the Hollywood studio, where the set was contained within a giant polythene bag to stop the birds crashing into the lights and equipment. 'Crows are the chimpanzees of birds. The hardest to train and catch are the hawks and eagles. You could teach them to hunt and kill, but they know it already. But you can't teach them any tricks.' Grips coaxed the birds back and forth across the set with food, and blasts of air were used to send the birds into a flurry of wild flapping. In some scenes the actors smeared their hands and faces with raw hamburger and waited for the birds to peck them. 'Birds make excellent heavies,' Hitchcock told *Time*. 'After all, they've been put in cages, shot at, and shoved into ovens for centuries. It's only natural they should fight back. Many people are terrified of them. Once the picture is released, it may do wonders for cat sales and the scarecrow market.'

A wise old owl sat on an oak;
The more he saw the less he spoke;
The less he spoke the more he heard;
Why aren't we like that wise old bird?

ANON

❛Many amateurs still think that when birds sing and hop around, they are being merry and affectionate. They are not, of course; they are being aggressive and demanding the price of a cup of coffee. As, however, human beings are soft at heart and in the head, I suppose we shall go on regarding this thing as a much loved garden bird, even when it beats on the window with its beak and tells you to get that goddam food on the bird table or else.❜

BRITISH JOURNALIST MILES KINGTON (1941–2008)

How did the blue tit craze of opening milk bottles catch on so fast?

Foil-topped milk bottles, delivered to Britain's doorsteps, were introduced in the 1920s and almost immediately blue tits started pecking through the lids to get to the cream on top, leaving ornithologists up and down Britain open-mouthed in astonishment. Groups of these ever-restless and inquisitive birds even started following milkmen on their rounds, while others would sit near a doorstep waiting for the daily delivery to which they had become accustomed. The trend quickly spread through the entire tit population, baffling birdwatchers, scientists and milkmen in equal measure. The big question was: given that most tits only lived a year or so, how on earth did they manage to pass on the good news to their family and friends? Some thought the knowledge was passed through the genes, but even the pioneers of genetic science knew that the milk-top phenomenon was spreading way too fast for evolution to have absorbed the new trick and passed it on to the next generation. Proper research soon showed that the birds were learning the knack through a combination of their own experiments and the sight of older birds doing it. The point was proved by observation of robins' behaviour: occasionally a robin was also seen to peck through the foil, but the habit never caught on amongst the wider robin population because, the boffins quickly worked out, the robin feeds alone, unobserved by its young. For the record, blue tits prefer full-fat milk to skimmed.

Hawk Roosting

I sit in the top of the wood, my eyes closed.
Inaction, no falsifying dream
Between my hooked head and hooked feet:
Or in sleep rehearse perfect kills and eat.

The convenience of the high trees!
The air's buoyancy and the sun's ray
Are of advantage to me;
And the earth's face upward for my inspection.

My feet are locked upon the rough bark.
It took the whole of Creation
To produce my foot, my each feather:
Now I hold Creation in my foot

Or fly up, and revolve it all slowly –
I kill where I please because it is all mine.
There is no sophistry in my body:
My manners are tearing off heads –
The allotment of death.
For the one path of my flight is direct
Through the bones of the living.
No arguments assert my right:

The sun is behind me.
Nothing has changed since I began.
My eye has permitted no change.
I am going to keep things like this.

ENGLISH POET TED HUGHES (1930–98)

Can birds really forecast the weather?

If Napoleon Bonaparte had had even a passing knowledge of bird behaviour, he might have thought twice about beginning his fateful retreat from Moscow in 1812, which ended in the almost complete destruction of the 500,000-strong Grande Armée. In truth, with his supplies almost exhausted and the city in ruins, he had little choice, but soon after leaving the Russian capital on 19 October, he should have been filled with foreboding by the sight of thousands of geese, cranes, storks and other migratory birds heading south and west. It was an unusually early departure to warmer climes for the birds, indicating that particularly harsh winter weather was on its way.

Birds can tell us a lot about imminent changes in the weather. Woodpeckers are sometimes called 'rain birds' after their habit of calling and drumming loudly before the heavens open. Swallows, swifts and martins feed on insects high in the sky during good weather, but when the air pressure starts to drop, the bugs drop down, pursued by our acrobatic summer visitors, telling us that rain and unsettled weather are on the way. Hence the old rhyme: 'Swallows high, staying dry / Swallows low, wet will blow.' Migratory birds can also sense impending changes in the weather, telling them whether or not to set off.

A little cock-sparrow sat on a green tree,
And he chirruped, he chirruped, so merry was he;
A naughty boy came with his wee bow and arrow,
Determined to shoot this little cock-sparrow.
'This little cock-sparrow shall make me a stew,
And his giblets shall make me a little pie, too.'
'Oh, no,' says the sparrow, 'I won't make a stew.'
So he flapped his wings and away he flew.

ENGLISH NURSERY RHYME

❝ Here I met with one of the most extraordinary phenomena that I ever saw, or heard of: – Mr. Sellers has in his yard a large Newfoundland dog, and an old raven. These have fallen deeply in love with each other, and never desire to be apart. The bird has learned the bark of the dog, so that few can distinguish them. She is inconsolable when he goes out; and, if he stays out a day or two, she will get up all the bones and scraps she can, and hoard them up for him till he comes back. ❞

JOHN WESLEY (1703–91)

~~~~~~

Western man has no need of more superiority over nature whether outside or inside. He has both in an almost devilish perfection. What he lacks is conscious recognition of his inferiority to the nature around and within him. He must learn that he may not do exactly as he wills. If he does not learn this, his own nature will destroy him.

CARL JUNG (1875–1961)

~~~~~~

Not so clever now, are we?

The Greek poet Aeschylus is supposed to have died when an eagle, mistaking his bald head for a rock on which it could crack open its supper, dropped a tortoise on him from a great height.

Some Geese

Every child who has the use
Of his senses knows a goose.
See them underneath the tree
Gather round the goose-girl's knee,
While she reads them by the hour
From the works of Schopenhauer.

How patiently the geese attend!
But do they really comprehend
What Schopenhauer's driving at?
Oh, not at all; but what of that?
Neither do I; neither does she;
And, for that matter, nor does he.

OLIVER HERFORD

The Battle to Survive

HOW BIRDS ARE COPING
IN A DAMAGED WORLD

Why is there so much doom and gloom about the future of the world's wildlife?

Wildlife habitats are fragile, miniature eco-systems and the food chains sustaining animals that live in them are delicate, neatly balanced structures. Both are highly vulnerable to change – and the change to the natural world in the course of the Industrial Age has been phenomenal, especially during the first half of the twentieth century. Most species of birds, mammals, insects and fish are struggling to come to terms with the momentous upheaval to the environment; many are threatened with extinction, many more are endangered. For millions of years, nature's creatures had nothing but themselves to fret about and even after man entered the scene in significant numbers a few thousand years ago, the natural world changed very little. But in the space of two hundred years or so man has caused an astonishing amount of havoc to the world he shares with other creatures, both deliberately and unwittingly. The situation has become so critical that the vast majority of scientists and other experts fear that, unless we take radical action and take it very, very soon, then nature – being a giant, interconnecting, interdependent network – will start to implode, rapidly disappearing into a vortex of decline and destruction. As far back as

1970, U Thant, then Secretary-General of the United Nations, said in a speech:

'As we watch the sun go down, evening after evening, through the smog across the poisoned waters of our native earth, we must ask ourselves seriously whether we really wish some future universal historian on another planet to say about us: "With all their genius and with all their skill, they ran out of foresight and air and food and water and ideas," or "They went on playing politics until their world collapsed around them."'

And today, the environment is in an even more perilous state than it was 40 years ago . . . Anyway, on a more cheerful note, um . . . er . . . oh, yes, the numbers of Dartford warbler in Dorset are on the up once more and City beat United at the weekend . . .

Still flying into battle for our birds

The Royal Society for the Protection of Birds (RSPB) is Europe's largest wildlife conservation organization. The charity has one million members, employs over 1,500 staff and has over 19,000 volunteers on its books. It was founded in Didsbury, a suburb of Manchester, in 1889, to protest against the use of great crested grebe skins and feathers in fashion clothing. 'The RSPB . . . was born in and of cruelty, has thrived on it for a hundred years, grown successful and prosperous in fear, loathing and pain. Without the propensity of men to exercise their power in a wantonly destructive way, the RSPB would go out of business,' wrote Tony Samstag in his history of the organization, *For the Love of Birds*.

How many birds have become extinct in modern times?

The rate of extinction has increased enormously since the late fifteenth century when European countries first began exploring and colonizing the world. A great deal of damage had already been done by Polynesians to ever-vulnerable island species in the Pacific, but the arrival in the New World of Europeans, with their guns and their animals, took the devastation to a new level. The very latest research suggests that the world has lost around 200 species of bird since the start of the sixteenth century, but several hundred more may have disappeared. That's an average of one species per year, a rate 100 times greater than the natural cycle that had existed for tens of millions of years up until then. Before the rise of man, approximately one bird species per century disappeared from the world. We have managed to kill off hundreds in a blink of history's eye and unless drastic action is taken in the next few years, the prospects for birds in the twenty-first century are looking even grimmer. A slew of recent reports by authoritative bodies suggest that between 10 and 20 per cent of bird species will disappear in the next 100 years as climate change and environmental degradation tighten their grip on the planet.

❝ I have very little to say regarding this bird [Haast's Eagle, now extinct] as I have only seen two of them, and being pushed with hunger, I ate the pair of them. Under the circumstances I would have eaten the last of the dodo. It is all very well for science, lifting up its hands in horror, at what I once heard called gluttony, but let science tramp through the Westland bush or swamps [of New Zealand], for two or three days without food, and find out what hunger is. Besides at the time, which was many years ago, I was not aware that it was an almost extinct bird. Had I known so, I would at least have skinned it and kept the head and feet. ❞

EXPLORER CHARLES EDWARD DOUGLAS (1840–1916)

Why have the numbers of many once common farmland birds slumped in the last century?

The situation is indeed dire, with some species pushed to the verge of extinction and many more into the endangered category. It's down to the way we have managed the land. Modern farming methods, together with the constant expansion of our towns and cities, have radically altered the British landscape in recent decades. Natural wildlife habitats, food sources, animal and insect populations up and down the country – and across the world – have been put under enormous pressure by the way man lives today. When links in the food chain are badly damaged or broken it has a far-reaching effect on other species. So, for example, more efficient farming techniques have meant there is less seed around after tilling, with dire consequences for dozens of species of seed-eating birds and small rodents. As their numbers fall off so do those of the predatory birds that

depend on them for their survival. The same applies to the use of insecticides. Kill the insects by spraying and you effectively kill – or at best banish from that area – those birds that live off insects and, in turn, those birds of prey and other predators that live off the insect-eating birds.

Mechanization has wreaked havoc among farmland birds and other wildlife. It's not just that there is less spillage of seed at harvest time; the possibility of covering his acreage more quickly has encouraged the farmer to widen the tracts of land over which he can sweep his harvester, tractor and crop sprayer. To create a big field a farmer must get rid of any natural obstacles including hedges, copses, ponds,

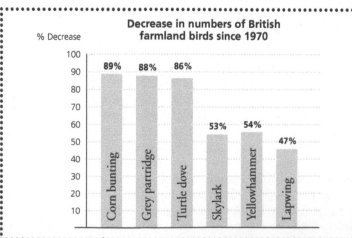

Decrease in numbers of British farmland birds since 1970

% Decrease

Corn bunting 89%
Grey partridge 88%
Turtle dove 86%
Skylark 53%
Yellowhammer 54%
Lapwing 47%

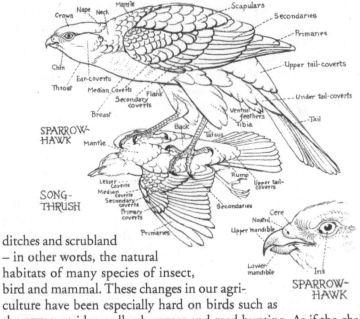

Crown
Nape
Neck
Mantle
Scapulars
Secondaries
Primaries
Chin
Ear-coverts
Throat
Median Coverts
Secondary coverts
Flank
Breast
Upper tail-coverts
Under tail-coverts
Ventral feathers
Tibia
Tail
SPARROW-HAWK
Mantle
Back
Tarsus
SONG-THRUSH
Lesser coverts
Median coverts
Secondary coverts
Primary coverts
Primaries
Rump
Upper tail-coverts
Secondaries
Cere
Nostril
Upper mandible
Lower mandible
Iris
SPARROW-HAWK

ditches and scrubland
– in other words, the natural
habitats of many species of insect,
bird and mammal. These changes in our agriculture have been especially hard on birds such as
the grey partridge, yellowhammer and reed bunting. As if the challenges weren't already tough enough, the European Commission announced plans to get rid of set-aside farmland without any accompanying plan to replace the benefits it brings to so many farmland birds. Many birds, including the skylark and the critically endangered stone curlew, use set-aside for food or nesting, or both. The RSPB and other conservation groups are calling on the politicians to ensure that farm subsidies are conditional on farmers leaving a small part of their land as set-aside.

Rejoice! A sparrowhawk has just eaten my blue tit!

A boom in the sparrowhawk population has caused a certain amount of consternation in the shires where some garden bird enthusiasts have been upset to see the small fast-flying predator swooping over their bird table and lawn to help itself to a mobile buffet of tits, finches and blackbirds. Females, which are 25 per cent larger than the slate-grey, orange-fronted males, are partial to a wood pigeon too. Like so many birds of prey, the sparrowhawk suffered a dramatic decline in the 1950s and 1960s as harmful pesticides worked their way up the food chain. Today, this small, secretive woodland hunter rivals the buzzard and kestrel as our most common bird of prey with over 40,000 pairs now resident in Britain.

A pair of sparrowhawks will kill at least 3,000 birds a year to feed themselves and their chicks, meaning that they are responsible for the deaths of over 120 million in total. This has led some to claim that the sparrowhawk is an unwelcome predator, as great a scourge as the domestic cat, and the bird's increasingly bad press has even prompted the RSPB to fly to its rescue with some PR interventions. The Royal Society has been at pains to point out that sparrowhawks are limited by the 'carrying capacity' of the habitat: in other words, the quantity of food and number of nesting sites in an area determines the number of sparrowhawks that can survive. Young sparrowhawks won't breed unless there's a territory available with sufficient food, so in years of high adult survival juveniles will struggle, since the birds tend not to travel more than 10 miles beyond the area where they were born. When the numbers of garden birds increase, sparrowhawk numbers will rise with them and when their numbers decline so do those of their predator.

This relationship between the sparrowhawk and its prey therefore is a very accurate barometer of the state of a local environment. Our common garden birds produce far more young every year than they need to maintain a healthy population, so sparrowhawks don't change the overall number that die, they just change the cause of death. So, next time you look out of the window to see a sparrowhawk pinning a blue tit to your lawn and pecking its heart out, you can relax, perhaps even break into joyful applause, in the knowledge that you are living in a very healthy eco-system.

Slaughter in the bird sanctuary

Over 50 per cent of New Zealand's native birds have become extinct since the first human settlers set foot on the islands somewhere around AD 900. Until then, the country was a giant bird sanctuary with no mammals there except for bats, which don't prey on birds. Without any predators to harass them, many birds had a perfect evolutionary excuse for dropping their guard. Why bother going to the energy-sapping effort of flying when there's nothing to fly away from

and all the food and shelter necessary is right there on the forest floor? Many birds became flightless and took to building their nests on the ground. When the first Polynesians stepped out of their canoes and came ashore, they would have been delighted to see thousands of giant moa birds, roaming the open plains and forests. The moa was a roast meal waiting to happen and by 1700 there were none left. They had all been killed, cooked, consumed and crapped into the undergrowth. Life got even worse for New Zealand's bird kingdom when the white man turned up with his guns, his rats, his cats and his eagerness to chop down the forests and plough the land to create fields for his crops and his cattle.

Where have all the barn owls gone?

It was only a couple of generations ago that farmers and gamekeepers slaughtered the barn owl because they thought it killed the young game birds they were breeding. It was soon realized that the owls' preference for mice, voles and rats helped control the rodent population on farms and the persecution stopped. But the birds faced an even bigger threat in the second half of the twentieth century when intensive farming saw their numbers halve within 50 years. The toxins in agricultural pesticides used in the 1950s were passed up the food chain, killing thousands of owls and countless other birds of prey. The destruction of thousands of miles of ancient hedgerows where mice and small birds lived has also contributed significantly to the decline in barn owl numbers. Some owls are killed when they fly into electricity cables, but, according to recent research by the Barn Owl Trust, starvation is the main cause of death today, with road casualties not far behind. Every year Britain's 4,000 pairs of barn owls produce roughly 12,000 young, 3,000 of which are killed on roads. Over 90 per cent of all barn owl road casualties are found dead on motorways and dual carriageways.

New species still out there

Every year or so the odd new species of bird is found in some dark corner of a distant forest, generally in the more remote areas of South America but also in other tropical regions such as southeast Asia (mainly Indonesia) and central Africa. The thrill of discovery, however, is dampened by the fact that the birds are invariably put straight on to the endangered species list.

The sad tale of the penguin of the north

Although it may well be joined by a number of others in the coming decades, so far the flightless great auk is the only British bird to have suffered the fate of global extinction. This large seabird that looked like a penguin crossed with a razorbill was once a common sight on our northern shores before our ancestors began clubbing, strangling and shooting it into oblivion. At first it was slaughtered for food, for its fat and for use as commercial fishing bait, but towards the end of its existence it was for its feathers and eggs that it was relentlessly harassed and finally exterminated. The feathers were used in fashion while the increasingly rare eggs found their way into collectors' display cabinets. The last great auk in the British Isles was killed on the island of St Kilda, off Scotland's west coast, in the summer of 1840. The last population of the great auk, which used to be found throughout the North Atlantic and was also called 'penguin' or 'gairfowl', lived on a volcanic island off southern Iceland, known as Geirfuglasker or 'Great Auk Rock'. On this island fortified by sheer cliffs all the way round, the birds were relatively safe from man's meddling and might well have survived for centuries longer. But in 1830, there was a volcanic episode under the sea and the island disappeared in an avalanche of tumbling rock, boiling water and clouds of steam. Was there nowhere safe on the planet for this beleaguered, defenceless bird? The great auk was a strong swimmer and the survivors of the volcanic catastrophe took to the water and found sanctuary on the nearby island of Eldey. Relief, however, was only temporary as the hunters were quick to locate and corner their prey. On 3 June 1844 the last pair was strangled to death and their egg crushed under the heel of a heavy boot.

The Victorian author Charles Kingsley was puzzled and upset by the extinction of the auk. He wrote about its demise in his 1863 children's classic *The Water-Babies*:

Once we were a great nation, and spread over all the Northern Isles. But men shot us so, and knocked us on the head, and took our eggs – why, if you will believe it, they say that on the coast of Labrador the sailors used to lay a plank from the rock on board the thing called their ship, and drive us along the plank by hundreds, till we tumbled down into the ship's waist in heaps; and then, I suppose, they ate us, the nasty fellows! Well – but – what was I saying? At last, there were none of us left, except on the old Gairfowlskerry, just off the Iceland coast, up which no man could climb. Even there we had no peace; for one day, when I was quite a young girl, the land rocked, and the sea boiled, and the

sky grew dark, and all the air was filled with smoke and dust, and down tumbled the old Gairfowlskerry into the sea. The dovekies and marrocks, of course, all flew away; but we were too proud to do that. Some of us were dashed to pieces, and some drowned; and those who were left got away to Eldey, and the dovekies tell me they are all dead now, and that another Gairfowlskerry has risen out of the sea close to the old one, but that it is such a poor flat place that it is not safe to live on: and so here I am left alone.

How many birds are killed by cats every year?

It is estimated that Britain's eight million cats kill between 50 and 80 million birds each year, which is a vast amount when you consider that the total population of nesting birds is roughly 150 million. (The last scientific effort at counting back in the mid-1970s estimated that there were 134 million birds and common-bird numbers have been more or less stable since then.) Fortunately, most of the birds killed are common garden species that produce broods far larger than they need to sustain a stable population. A decent proportion of those taken by Socks and Tigger will be ones made weak through illness, starvation or injury, to which they would have anyhow succumbed. The other principal causes of death among birds are predation by other creatures, such as sparrowhawks and foxes, and flying into solid objects – windows chiefly.

Alarming bird facts

- One in eight of the world's birds – over a thousand species in total – face extinction. Of those, 190 are Critically Endangered.

- Farmland birds in Europe have declined by about 50 per cent in the last 50 years.

- 67 per cent of globally threatened birds on ocean islands are endangered by alien invasive species.

- Agricultural expansion and intensification threaten 50 per cent of Important Bird Areas in Africa.

- 43 per cent of Africa's Important Bird Areas have no legal recognition or protection.

- 64 per cent of globally threatened birds, most of them in the tropics, are threatened by unsustainable forestry.

- Conservation investment is over 20 times higher in developed than developing countries.

(BIRDLIFE INTERNATIONAL AND THE INTERNATIONAL UNION FOR THE CONSERVATION OF NATURE)

It is a melancholy reflection, that, from man, downwards, to the smallest living creature, all are found to prey upon and devour each other. The philosophic mind, however, sees this waste of animal life again and again repaired by fresh stores, ever ready to supply the void, and the great work of generation and destruction perpetually going on, and to this dispensation of an all-wise Providence, so interesting to humanity, bows in awful silence.

THOMAS BEWICK (1753–1828)

President Teddy Roosevelt was a key figure in the early years of the conservation movement, forcing through a raft of laws to protect birds in the United States during his eight-year term of office at the start of the twentieth century. He was also responsible for the establishment of 53 Federal Wildlife Refuges across the country, as well as 18 areas of special interest and 40 million acres of national forests. In his earlier incarnation as governor of New York, he forced the closure of factories trading in bird feathers.

A tale of two doves

Its numbers having increased hugely since 1970, the collared dove is now one of the most common birds in Britain. It bred in Britain for the first time in 1955 (in Cromer, Norfolk) having spread rapidly across Europe from its traditional home in the eastern Mediterranean in the first half of the twentieth century. It owes much of its success as a species to the fact that, like the pigeon, it is not an especially fussy feeder. The smaller, more attractive turtle dove, by contrast, has seen its numbers plummet by 86 per cent in the last 30 years and is now on the Red List of endangered species. In common with other farmland species this attractive summer visitor with striking mottled plumage has struggled with loss of habitat and fewer sources of seed, but it's not entirely clear why its numbers have fallen quite so steeply. A great number are shot in the Mediterranean, especially in Malta, during migration. Prolonged droughts in Africa have not helped their cause either.

Newsflash: the dodo is still extinct

The dodo was the first recorded of the many bird species killed off by man. Found only on the previously uninhabited island of Mauritius in the Indian Ocean, the dodo had, over time, become flightless because there were no land-based predators from which it needed to flee into the air. For tens of millions of years the dodos built their nests on the ground and happily waddled around their island paradise munching on fruit, rearing their young and minding their own business. And then man came ashore. After its discovery by the Portuguese in 1598, sailors started to use Mauritius as a port of call to stock up on food and water and carry out repairs on their ships. Plump, fleshy birds, bigger than turkeys, that couldn't fly away were easy prey for man, his dogs and his egg-eating pigs and monkeys. In 1681, less than a century after the species encountered its first human being, the last dodo on earth was clubbed to death by a hungry sailor. All that remains of the dodo today is a head and foot at Oxford University, a foot in London's British Museum, a head in Copenhagen, plus a few bones scattered around museums in Europe and the United States.

What is the true state of British bird populations?

Trying to establish a clear, accurate picture about how our 500 species of birds are faring in the modern world can be a confusing business. Media reports often appear to contradict one another with one newspaper article painting a gloomy picture, another alleging that the future's all rosy and marvellous; one survey says numbers are up, another that they're down. Broadly speaking, this is the current situation:

- In the two or three decades up to 1970 many species suffered sharp declines.
- Since 1970, most common bird numbers have been roughly stable.
- Most birds of prey and a handful of other endangered species are making a comeback, thanks to conservation projects and legislation.
- Garden birds are doing well owing to the growing popularity of feeding them.
- Birds of our farmland and our woodland and long-distance migrants are in big trouble.
- Conservation bodies and projects need far greater help from government to secure the future of dozens of threatened species.

The length of time over which a survey looks at the trends is another crucial factor and the experts now differentiate between long-term (from 1970 to the present) and short-term (from 1994). The confusion often arises when one media report uses the long-term trend, and another the short-term. The annual Breeding Bird Survey, run by the British Trust for Ornithology, the Royal Society for the Protection of Birds and the Joint Nature Conservation Committee, provides the most accurate snapshot of the state of our birds. The table below gives the trends for a selection of common breeding birds, as published in 2008; the species shown have been chosen to highlight how the confusion arises:

Type of bird	Long-term % change (1970–2006)	Short-term % change (1994–2007)
Blackbird	− 16	+ 24
Collared dove	+ 387	+ 27
Blue tit	+ 33	+ 14
Song thrush	− 50	+ 18
Magpie	+ 96	0
Starling	− 73	− 26
Tree sparrow	− 93	+ 15
Sparrowhawk	+ 106	− 12
House martin	− 35	+ 9
Goldcrest	−17	+ 50

Birds and bulldozers

Birds have learned to live in every habitat on earth, from the frozen
ice caps of the polar regions to the scorching heat of the desert, from
mountain ranges to wetlands, coastlines, scrub, cities and parks. But
three quarters of the world's 10,000 bird species live in the forests,
especially the humid, damp forests of the tropics that cover just 5
per cent of the world's land surface. As the rainforests recoil at the
advance of the bulldozer, the number of species and the number of
individual birds shrink in proportion; and the rate of extinction is set
to accelerate sharply because many tropical species have very small
breeding areas.

Let us prey

One tenth of the world's bird species are congregatory, including a
great number of waterbirds and migrants, gathering together into
large, spectacular colonies to nest, breed, feed, roost or migrate.
Living in a colony has many advantages, including greater safety from
predators and sharing information about food sources, but it also
makes these species extremely vulnerable to environmental degradation, especially when large numbers of birds make use of just a few
important sites. Indeed, some 20 per cent of these species are cat-
egorized as 'globally threatened'.

The future is red for 67 British birds

If a bird species is under serious threat it ends up on the Red List of
the International Union for the Conservation of Nature (IUCN),
the world's most authoritative conservation body whose information
is supplied by hundreds of government agencies and international
organizations. There are currently 67 species of British birds (roughly
10 per cent of the total) on the Red List and 121 on the Amber List.
A bird can be placed on the Red List for one of four reasons:

  a) It is globally threatened.
  b) It has suffered a historical decline since 1800.
  c) There has been a rapid decline (over 50 per cent) in the
      UK breeding population over the last 25 years.
  d) There has been a rapid contraction (over 50 per cent)
      of its breeding range over the last 25 years.

British birds on the dreaded Red List

White-fronted goose	Tree sparrow	Kittiwake
Ringed plover	Black grouse	Ring ouzel
Golden oriole	Red-necked	Twite
Nightingale	phalarope	Slavonian grebe
Pochard	Grasshopper warbler	Herring gull
Dotterel	Yellow wagtail	Fieldfare
Red-backed shrike	Capercaillie	Lesser redpoll
Pied flycatcher	Woodcock	White-tailed eagle
Scaup	Savi's warbler	Turtle dove
Whimbrel	Grey wagtail	Song thrush
Willow tit	Grey partridge	Yellowhammer
Black redstart	Arctic skua	Hen harrier
Long-tailed duck	Aquatic warbler	Cuckoo
Curlew	Tree pipit	Redwing
Marsh tit	Balearic shearwater	Cirl bunting
Whinchat	Puffin	Corncrake
Common scoter	Marsh warbler	Lesser spotted
Black-tailed godwit	Hawfinch	woodpecker
Skylark	Shag	Mistle thrush
House sparrow	Roseate tern	Corn bunting
Velvet scoter	Starling	Lapwing
Ruff	Linnet	Merlin
Wood warbler	Red-necked grebe	Spotted flycatcher

Why we should all be alarmed by the recent sharp decline in bird populations

Like canaries down a mine alerting miners of old to a gas leak, the birds of today are sending out messages of foreboding about our poisoned, damaged world. Birds, as a whole group, are more sensitive to changes in their environment than other animals, so when they start falling off perches we should all be troubled. They are in the forwardmost trench of nature's resistance against the relentless attrition of environmental degradation. Our birds are nature's early warning system and the scientists are telling us that if we don't start acting on their distress signals, it won't be long before the rest of the animal world is overrun as well. The populations of many species are declining rapidly because habitats are being destroyed or undermined, food sources are disappearing and, tricked by the increasingly weird and erratic weather, the birds' migration and breeding patterns are changing. In short, birds are confused and under stress. Just because you can hear your robins, blue tits and sparrows chirping away happily in the garden every morning, don't be fooled into thinking that all is well in 'birdworld'.

The impact of global warming, whatever its cause, has already started to have its effect on migratory birds. Summer visitors to Britain are arriving in their breeding areas two to three weeks earlier than thirty years ago and as winters become even milder and spring arrives earlier and earlier, the birds will be fooled into setting off earlier and arriving at their summer residences before their food sources are ready. Those that winter in sub-Saharan Africa are likely to experience mounting problems as conditions get hotter and drier and the boundaries of the desert creep ever outwards. As the planet heats up, the ice retreats and the snowcaps melt, Arctic and montane species become ever more vulnerable. For cold-weather British birds such as the ptarmigan and the snow bunting, the future looks especially bleak. Enjoy them while they last because the ornithologists

tell us they are likely to disappear in under a generation. Warmer seas and overfishing are having a devastating effect on marine stocks, which in turn is having a domino effect on seabird populations.

> My left arm ached from lifting my gun, my shoulder from the recoil, and I was deaf and stunned from the banging . . . When in the late afternoon the carnage stopped almost 4,000 pheasants had been killed. The bright limp carcasses were laid out in rows of 100; the whole place was littered with feathers and spent cartridges.

Edward VIII, then Prince of Wales, on a shooting party on the Buckinghamshire estate of Lord Burnham in 1913. His father, George V, suggested that the party had 'perhaps gone too far'.

How did the world's most abundant bird become extinct within 100 years?

In 1813 a flock of over a billion passenger pigeons measuring 300 miles long and three miles wide took four days to pass overhead, darkening the skies like a giant eclipse as it made its way across the United States. It is estimated that there were five billion passenger pigeons in North America at this time. By the start of the First World War, when man turned his talents for mass killing onto himself, not a single bird of the species was left. The natural enemies of the passenger pigeon were hawks, owls, weasels, skunks and tree snakes, but their combined threat was as nothing compared to the greed and cruelty of man.

The birds were a good source of cheap meat for slaves and the poor. Settlers, heading further and further west, began slaughtering the long-tailed birds in their millions and selling them in city markets. After a gradual decline, their numbers collapsed between 1870 and 1890. Ornithologist and artist John James Audubon recorded how three million pigeons were sold by a single market hunter in the year 1878. Recent studies suggest that loss of habitat, caused by settlers clearing the land, was also a significant factor in the birds' decline. The settlers were extraordinarily inventive in the ways they found to exterminate the pigeons, many using giant nets to trap them before killing them by crushing their skulls with their thumbs.

On 1 September 1914, the bird became officially extinct when Martha, the last known survivor of the species, died in Cincinnati Zoo. Martha, named after the wife of former President George Washington, was preserved in a block of ice and sent to the Smithsonian Institution where she was stuffed and mounted on a perch. In Wyalusing State Park in Wisconsin, a monument to the passenger pigeon reads: 'This species became extinct through the avarice and thoughtlessness of man.' But its rapid and dramatic disappearance was not all in vain as it drew attention to the issue of man's relationship with the natural world, and provided a huge spur to the fledgling conservation movement.

Wet tits

It wasn't just Britain's humans who had to endure the relentlessly wet and miserable summer of 2007. Many common British birds suffered a catastrophic breeding season with the chicks of seven species struggling to survive in the crucial first few weeks of life. Blue tits suffered their worst breeding season on record, down almost 50 per cent on the year before, with a staggering 10 million chicks killed off by a shortage of food, caused by the torrential rain, according to the British Trust for Ornithology (BTO). With climatologists predicting increasingly wet summers in the century ahead, the outlook is, you could say, bleak and unsettled for many of our birds. (The figures for the equally wet summer of 2008 were unavailable at the time of writing.) There are about 3.5 million blue tit pairs in Britain and although they only need one or two of their large broods to go on to breed to maintain a stable population, a succession of wet summers would lead to a huge crash in their numbers and one of the most common species could quickly find its way on to the endangered list. The average clutch is six but there can be as many as 10 chicks in a blue tit brood – the vast majority of which will never make it into a second year – and each one needs 100 caterpillars. As the rains fell from the sky day after day, the caterpillars either failed to appear or they were washed off their host plants, leaving the parent blue tits unable to provide for their young. Many of those that did receive sufficient nutrition and managed to fledge, then died of hypothermia as their thin, downy plumage was no protection against the prolonged drenching. The great tit also suffered in the deluge with its numbers down by 33 per cent, while the reed warbler was down 27 per cent and the whitethroat by 25 per cent.

The Darkling Thrush

I leant upon a coppice gate
  When Frost was spectre-gray,
And Winter's dregs made desolate
  The weakening eye of day.
The tangled bine-stems scored the sky
  Like strings of broken lyres, '
And all mankind that haunted nigh
  Had sought their household fires.

The land's sharp features seemed to be
  The Century's corpse outleant,
His crypt the cloudy canopy,
  The wind his death-lament.
The ancient pulse of germ and birth
  Was shrunken hard and dry,
And every spirit upon earth
  Seemed fervourless as I.

At once a voice arose among
  The bleak twigs overhead
In a full-hearted evensong
  Of joy illimited;
An aged thrush, frail, gaunt, and small,
  In blast-beruffled plume,
Had chosen thus to fling his soul
  Upon the growing gloom.

So little cause for carolings
  Of such ecstatic sound
Was written on terrestrial things
  Afar or nigh around,
That I could think there trembled through
  His happy good-night air
Some blessed Hope, whereof he knew
  And I was unaware.

ENGLISH NOVELIST AND POET THOMAS HARDY (1840–1928)

Written on the eve of the new century and published in *The Times* on New Year's Day, 1901, 'The Darkling Thrush' captures the ambivalent feelings people had about the new modern epoch they were entering, leaving behind the certainties of the Victorian Age.

The troubled history of the peregrine falcon

A peregrine falcon stooping at full pelt to kill its prey in mid-air is one of nature's great spectacles, but it is a fairly rare sight these days. The peregrine may well be the fastest creature on the planet, clocking 180 mph as it stoops to conquer, and one of the most adaptable, but it has never been speedy or wily enough to escape the attentions of human beings. Prized for its falconry skills for centuries, this powerful, usually solitary bird has endured a dreadful 100 years or so in which it has been driven to the brink of extinction in Britain, mainland Europe and North America. Found on every continent in all manner of habitats, from steepling mountains to flat coastal plains, from tropical forests to semi-desert and scrub, the peregrine has proved to be one of the world's most successful species – until very recently. In the first half of the twentieth century it was persecuted by gamekeepers and landowners worried about their stocks of game birds. In the Second World War, thousands were killed to protect homing pigeons carrying important military messages, but its numbers had recovered by 1955 after new legislation outlawed its killing. Soon afterwards, though, the population began to plummet as fast as the bird itself takes its prey, crashing altogether in some parts of England and Wales where it fed off birds on agricultural land. By 1962 there were only 68 pairs left in Britain, a minuscule fraction of its natural number. Numbers of other birds of prey began to tumble as well and the causes of the dramatic decline remained a mystery until research scientists discovered that new agricultural pesticides were to blame. Organochloride chemicals were moving up the food chain, causing the shells of the peregrines' eggs to become thinner so that they would break when incubated by the adult. Thanks to a ban on the harmful pesticides and the efforts of conservationists, the situation has improved significantly and peregrine numbers have climbed. There are currently a healthy 1,500 pairs in the UK, many of them nesting in city cathedrals and tower blocks, which serve as perfect alternatives to the cliffs where they were once found in great numbers.

If you go down to the woods today, you're in for a bad surprise ...

We haven't quite reached the point where we're more likely to find a Teddybears' picnic in the local woods than catch a glimpse or song of some of our previously common woodland birds, but ornithologists have been astounded to discover that their numbers have been crashing in recent years. Worse still, they don't understand why. Between 1994 and 2007, nightingale numbers were down by 60 per cent, spotted flycatchers by 59 per cent, willow tits by 77 per cent, pied flycatchers by 54 per cent and wood warblers by 67 per cent, while the lesser spotted woodpecker has declined so fast that it is off the monitoring scale.

Bambi, I'm sorry to report, is one of the main suspects and is currently under investigation. (Unfortunately, he's exercising his right to silence which is delaying the inquiries.) Most species of deer, notably the little muntjac, have been increasing over the same period that the birds have been disappearing. Deer live in the woods too and it is thought that their constant foraging and prancing about through the undergrowth is damaging nesting sites. Another cause, at least in part, is the disappearance of the shrub layer, caused by changes in woodland management and the decline in traditional coppicing. The main problem, however, may turn out to lie thousands of miles away in sub-Saharan Africa where the evidence is growing that all is not well for our migrant birds. Four of the five woodland birds showing the steepest drop are summer visitors while eight out of ten of the species suffering the greatest decline in all British birds are long-distance migrants. This suggests that either the birds are encountering difficulties on their journey to and from Africa, or that their habitat there has been compromised.

British birds showing major increases in recent years

Wood pigeon	Carrion crow
Collared dove	Greenfinch
Magpie	Goldfinch
Red kite	Raven
Greater spotted woodpecker	Sparrowhawk
Pheasant	
Swallow	
Blackcap	
Great tit	
Nuthatch	
Jackdaw	

The wholesale slaughter of the albatross

For centuries, an albatross following a ship has been seen as a good omen. It was believed that the birds carried the souls of dead sailors, watching over the ship and crew. If there is any truth in the sailors' superstition that to kill or injure an albatross brings bad luck, then the crews of the world's long-line fishing fleets are in for some serious ill fortune.

British naturalist Sir David Attenborough is just one of many high-profile public figures who have added their voices to the increasingly urgent campaign to save the albatross from impending disaster. 'Albatrosses have survived in the harshest marine environments for 50 million years; more than 100 times longer than our own species,' he said recently. 'However, these magnificent birds are unable to cope with man-made threats, such as long-line fishing.'

Nineteen of the world's 22 albatross species, as well as storm petrels and shearwaters, are seriously threatened by 'long-lining', a form of intensive fishing where lines measuring up to 80 miles long are fitted with thousands and thousands of baited hooks. The lines are pulled through the oceans, many of them by pirate fishing crews, in search of highly lucrative catches such as tuna, swordfish and Patagonian toothfish that will fetch hundreds of thousands of dollars.

Seeing flocks of other birds feeding off the discarded fish waste and bait from a commercial fishing boat, the albatrosses are drawn to these death-traps like bees to a honey pot. The baited lines, thrown overboard by the fishermen, float for a few fatal minutes before sinking beneath the waves. The albatross, an expert at feeding off the water's surface, swoops to take the bait. Immediately the large hook rips into the throat and as the line starts to sink the choking albatross is dragged under to a hideous death.

Once they have reached maturity (between 7 and 12 years), most species of albatross will breed every other year as it takes the better part of 12 months to incubate the one egg and raise the chick. When an albatross fails to return to the family nest, the chick will die. Left to themselves, the birds live for 60 years but they are currently being killed in such huge numbers that they can't breed fast enough to keep up with the rate of their extermination. Conservative estimates put

the annual death toll at 100,000, meaning one albatross dies every five minutes. While you are reading this, one of the world's oldest and most majestic birds will be having its throat torn out by a giant hook.

Simple ways for fishermen to halt the slaughter of the albatross

- Use colourful plastic streamers suspended over the long lines at the back of the boat to scare birds away from baited hooks.
- Use underwater chutes to let out the long lines.
- Use blue-dyed bait to make it hard for the birds to see it.
- Lay fishing lines at night.
- Add weights to fishing lines so the baited hooks sink faster.

In addition to these practical steps the commercial fishing enterprises can take themselves, government action is needed to stamp out pirate fishing.

Undefended coastline

Conservation groups are furious that the British government will not bestow greater protection on marine wildlife sites that are home to 18 species of fish, mammal, bird or reptile considered at risk of global extinction. They point out the glaring discrepancy between the treatment of marine and inland sites – all the more frustrating given that only three such endangered species depend on land or fresh-water habitats. The UK's coastline hosts huge populations of waterbirds that are reckoned to be the country's greatest contribution to global biodiversity. The great skua, Manx shearwater, gannet and shag have their most important populations in the world on Britain's coasts, while the puffin, kittiwake and guillemot also rely on British waters for breeding. In the future, campaigners insist, even greater demands will be placed upon an already highly fragile marine environment. Under European law, the UK has protected only three marine sites of importance to birds, fewer than tiny Latvia, even though the UK's coastline is 25 times longer.

> *In many ways, the alba-*
> *tross may be the*
> *ultimate test of whether*
> *or not, as a species our-*
> *selves, we are serious*
> *about conservation:*
> *capable of co-existing on*
> *this planet with other*
> *species. Or are we going*
> *to sacrifice what's left of*
> *wisdom on the altar of*
> *short-term gain?*
>
> THE PRINCE OF WALES
> (1949–)

Preying on vultures

Ninety-nine per cent of the three species of vultures found in southern Asia have been wiped out through the use of a veterinary drug called Diclofenac, and there are fears that African vultures will go the same way unless the drug is banned.

The vultures suffer kidney failure when they feed on the carcasses of domesticated animals that have been treated with the drug. In 2006, the governments of India, Pakistan and Nepal banned the manufacture of the drug in the first stage of phasing it out, but numbers of vultures are so low that their survival as a species now depends on captive breeding programmes. Stamping out the drug completely will be difficult as it has been produced by hundreds of different manufacturers and sold under dozens of names. It is currently being used by vets in a number of African countries to the alarm of conservationists, who have pointed out that there are perfectly safe alternatives while reminding governments that vultures do more good than harm, clearing the land of disease-ridden carcasses and keeping down the population of rabies-carrying feral dogs.

Global warming: now the good news

The Dartford warbler may sound like a Cockney music-hall crooner, but this secretive bird of the low heathland, whose numbers have been steadily recovering in recent years, hails originally from the Mediterranean. It suffers terribly in extremely cold winters and almost disappeared from Britain following the savage winter of 1962/63 when its resident population collapsed from 450 pairs to single figures. A sparrow-like bird with a dark red breast and a distinctive orange ring around its eyes, the Dartford warbler is one of the British birds to be benefiting from our steadily warming climate and there are now over 3,000 pairs breeding in southern England.

Why ptarmigans are in a flap

Already threatened by global warming and the gradual disappearance of the few pockets of Alpine habitat left in Britain, the ptarmigan is also under growing stress from an unwitting alliance of sheep, foxes, crows and tourists. Sheep have grazed out areas of heather and bilberry in the Scottish Highlands, destroying vital food sources for the bird. The ptarmigan turns from grey or brown in the summer months to a striking total white in the winter, giving it year-round camouflage from birds of prey. However, foxes and crows, which are drawn to areas where sheep mortality is high to feed off the carcasses, have also been attacking incubating ptarmigans and their nests during their forays up the mountain. Humans aren't helping the bird's cause either. Walkers and climbers have been leaving more rubbish in recent years, giving the scavengers further incentive to forage in the ptarmigans' traditional habitat.

Why are there never any birds to be found in Britain's evergreen forests?

Er . . . what evergreen forests? Until roughly 500 BC, 90 per cent of Britain was covered in woodland, much of it evergreen, but over the years the plough and the bulldozer have turned our environment into an almost completely man-made landscape – and that includes the Highlands of Scotland. All that heather and grim bleak beauty of the mountains was created by man! There are only a handful of natural evergreen forests left and in fact there are plenty of birds to be found living in them. Where you won't find many birds is in the evergreen plantation forests created by man for commercial purposes, made up of non-native species that don't appeal to our insects, forcing our insectivore birds to forage elsewhere for their meals. Another factor is that these plantations are dark, forbidding places where the tightly packed ranks and columns of trees let in so little light that little else can grow on the forest floor. They do have some attractions for our birds, however. A number of species, especially finches, use the forests as dormitories, attracted by the safety of the dense foliage. Greater spotted woodpeckers, coal tits, goldcrests and firecrests – Britain's smallest birds – the chubby brick-red crossbill, yellow-bibbed siskin and the turkey-like capercaillie, now virtually extinct in Britain, make up the majority of the small number of birds that will spend the day in these otherwise unwelcoming environments.

Why has the sparrow completely disappeared from our cities in recent years?

The house sparrow was once a more common sight than the pigeon in central London and other large British cities. In the days before the automobile, our towns and cities hosted enormous sparrow populations that lived off the waste grain from horse feed. Their numbers began to decline in the first half of the twentieth century as cars gradually took over from horses as the principal – if slightly slower – means of urban transport. These audacious, jaunty little birds were still a common sight in the late 1980s – but suddenly they vanished. By the new millennium there were none to be found. Quite why they have disappeared so abruptly remains something of a mystery. In 2001, a newspaper – the *Independent* – offered a prize of £5,000 for the first scientific paper published in a serious journal to explain the phenomenon, but at the time of writing the prize remains unclaimed. Numbers of house sparrows in Britain as a whole have declined by 50 per cent – up to 90 per cent in some areas – in the last 15 years and now European cities are also starting to report dramatic declines. Possible explanations include: the disappearance of insects vital to sparrow chicks in their first days of life; an as yet unidentified disease that's sweeping the sparrow world; increasing numbers of other birds such as the pigeon, blackbird and jay, who hog the best nesting sites; tighter building regulations and home improvements eradicating gaps and crevices where sparrows like to nest; increase in numbers of predators such as cats, magpies and kestrels; climate change, pesticides, pollutions . . . The list runs on and on. The hot money is on the disappearing insects as the cause but the truth may well turn out to be a combination of all or many of these factors.

from **The Rime of the Ancient Mariner**

'The ice was here, the ice was there,
The ice was all around:
It crack'd and growl'd, and roar'd and howl'd,
Like noises in a swound!

At length did cross an Albatross,
Thorough the fog it came;
As if it had been a Christian soul,
We hail'd it in God's name.

It ate the food it ne'er had eat,
And round and round it flew.
The ice did split with a thunder-fit;
The helmsman steer'd us through!

And a good south wind sprung up behind;
The Albatross did follow,
And every day, for food or play,
Came to the mariners' hollo!

In mist or cloud, on mast or shroud,
It perch'd for vespers nine;
Whiles all the night, through fog-smoke white,
Glimmer'd the white moonshine.'

'God save thee, ancient Mariner,
From the fiends, that plague thee thus! –
Why look'st thou so?' – 'With my crossbow
I shot the Albatross.'

SAMUEL TAYLOR COLERIDGE

REFERENCES AND ACKNOWLEDGEMENTS

Addison, Joseph, *Spectator*.

Alexander, H. G., *Seventy Years of Birdwatching*, Poyser, 1974.

Allen, Glover Morrill, 'Birds and Their Attributes' from *The Bedside Book of Birds* by Graeme Gibson, Marshall Jones Company, 1925.

Beeton, Mrs, *Beeton's Book of Household Management*, Wordsworth, 2008.

Bewick, Thomas, *A History of British Birds*, 1816.

BirdLife International and the International Union for the Conservation of Nature.

Brontë, Anne, 'Views of Life' from *The Complete Poems of Anne Brontë*, ed. Clement Shorter and Charles W. Hatfield, Kessinger Publishing, 2008.

Deval, Jacques, 'Afin de vivre bel et bien'.

Ellis, Havelock, *Impressions and Comments*, Houghton Mifflin, 1918.

Fisher, James, *Watching Birds*, Penguin, 1941.

Fisher, James and Lockley, Robert, *Sea Birds: An Introduction to the Natural History of the Sea-Birds of the North Atlantic*, Collins, 1954.

Freud, Clement, *Freud on Food*, 1978.

Genesis 8:6–12, New American Standard Bible, 1995.

Hudson, W. H., *British Birds*, 1895.

Hughes, Ted, 'Hawk Roosting' from *Collected Poems of Ted Hughes*, Faber & Faber, 2005.

Jung, Carl, *Psychology and Religion*, Yale University Press, 1977.

Kington, Miles, *Nature Made Ridiculously Simple*, Penguin, 1983.

Langland, William, *Piers Plowman*, Penguin Books, 1959.

Lanier, Sidney, 'The Owl Against the Robin' from *Poems*, ed. Mary D. Lanier, BiblioBazaar, 2007.

Lawrence, D. H., 'Self-pity' from *The Complete Poems of D. H. Lawrence*, Wordsworth Editions Limited, 1994, reproduced by permission of Pollinger Limited and The Estate of Frieda Lawrence Ravagli.

Longfellow, Henry Wadsworth, *Evangeline: A Tale of Arcadie*, Biblio Bazaar, 2008.

Longfellow, Henry Wadsworth, *Hyperion: A Romance*, Dodo Press, 2008.

Meiklejohn, M. F. M., 'Wild Birds as Human Food', *Proceedings of the Nutrition Society*, Vol. 21, 1962.

Merritt, Dixon Lanier, 'The Pelican'.

Nicholson, Max, *The Art of Birdwatching*, H. F. & G. Witherby, 1931.

Peattie, Donald Culross, *Singing in the Wilderness*, G. P. Putnam's Sons, 1935.

Pope, Alexander, 'Windsor Forest' from *Selected Poetry: Alexander Pope*, Oxford University Press, 1998.

RSPB Big Garden Birdwatch, 2007.

Service, Robert, 'Bird Watcher' from *Collected Poems of Robert Service*, Warner Books, 1993.

Thomson, James, *The Seasons*, 1805.

Thoreau, Henry David, *Walden, or Life in the Woods*, Dover Publications, 1995.

Wesley, John, *Journal*, 1790.

White, Gilbert, *Natural History and Antiquities of Selborne*, 1789.

Whitman, Walt, 'The Dalliance of Eagles' from *Leaves of Grass*, Everyman, 1993.

Wordsworth, William, 'The Recluse – Book First' from *Home at Grasmere*, Penguin Books, 1986.

Wordsworth, William, 'The Solitary Reaper' from *William Wordsworth: Selected Poetry*, Oxford University Press, 1998.

Young, Roland, *Not For Children*, Garden City Publishing, 1945.

http://bestiary.ca

It takes a small army of people to produce a book like this. Editors, copy-editors, illustrators, designers and proof-readers, backed up by squadrons of assistants, all play a crucial part in ensuring the book is fit to go to the printers. It has been my good fortune that Transworld Publishers have a superbly professional team to pave my way and clear up the mess I leave in my wake. So thanks in particular to Susanna Wadeson and then, in alphabetical order, to Deborah Adams, Hugh Adams, Lucy Davey, Elizabeth Dobson, Geraldine Ellison, Manpreet Grewal, Phil Lord, Richard Shailer and Katrina Whone. Thanks as always to Araminta Whitley at literary agents Lucas Alexander Whitley (LAW) and to my friend Steve Apps for his patience in pointing out and describing all the different species living within binocular range of my home. I reserve most of my gratitude, however, for my sister-in-law Olivia Pemberton who inspired me to write the book. Without her curiosity and enthusiasm, the project would never have taken wing.

INDEX

albatrosses 38, 89, 121,
    195–7, 201–2
    wandering albatross
    23–4, 69
Archaeopteryx 1, 4–5,
    11
Arctic skuas 149–50
Arctic terns 129–30
Argentine lake ducks
    72
Australian black swans
    22

bar-headed geese 126
barn owls 77, 79,
    179–80
barnacle geese 132–3
beaks 65–8, 82–3
bearded tits 146
bee-eaters 79
behaviour of birds
    144–61
Bewick's swan 16–17
binoculars 124–5
bird food see feeding
    birds
bird song 46–53, 54–8,
    164–6
bird statistics 40–1
birds of prey 30, 36
black vultures 62, 81,
    90–1
blackbirds 13, 32, 42,
    89, 186
    behaviour 151, 152,
    154, 160
    song 50, 58, 164
black-headed gulls 150
blackpoll warblers 132
blue tits 42, 169, 186,
    191–2

body temperature 18,
    60, 69, 126
bower-birds 34–6, 164
brains 162
breeding 13–20, 47,
    186
Brent geese 137
British birds 29
bustards 122
buzzards 135

caged birds 88,
    109–10, 138
calls 47, 48, 164–6
camouflage 3, 27, 199
Canada geese 90
capercaillies 99, 200
cassowaries 152
chickens 61, 63, 76,
    120
    see also hens
chicks see raising young
chinstrap penguins 23
coal tits 42, 200
coastlines 36–7, 149,
    153, 197
collared doves 42, 48,
    184, 186
colonies 22, 31–2, 149,
    153, 187
common gulls 150
condors 81
coots 29
cormorants 4, 71, 80,
    84–6, 99
courtship 3, 15, 17, 19,
    33–4, 68
cranes 9, 19, 171
crossbills 200
crows 98–9, 154, 163,
    168

cuckoos 28–9, 89, 99
    migration 127–8,
    137

Dartford warblers
    198–9
dawn chorus 48–9, 52
death 16, 38, 158–9,
    182
    see also extinctions
digestion 63, 70
dippers 158
display see courtship
dodos 184–5
doves 6, 44, 89, 184
    see also collared doves
drinking 70, 75
ducks 21, 69, 72
    eggs 103
    flight 96, 122
    plumage 71, 73–4,
    79–80
dunlin 98
dunnocks 24–6, 42, 43
dusting 150–1

eagles 77, 99, 114–15,
    135, 168, 172
edible birds 61
eggs 16, 27–8, 33, 62
    cooking and eating
    102, 104
egrets 96
eider ducks 79–80
emperor penguins
    31–2, 60–1, 121
evolution of birds 1–6,
    9–10, 11–12
extinctions 174–5,
    178–9, 187
    dodos 184–5

extinctions (*cont.*)
  great auks 180–1
  passenger pigeons
    190–1
eyes 75–8, 81

faeces 70, 73, 88
farmland habitats
  175–7, 179
fat 64–5
feathers 3, 62, 64
  see also moulting;
  plumage
feeding birds 42–5,
  101, 111, 126
  cleaning feeders 59
feral pigeons 5–6
fieldfares 148–9
fighting 20, 145,
  155–7, 157
finches 42, 66, 126,
  154, 200
firecrests 200
flamingos 66, 74
flight 64, 112–26
  see also migration
flightless birds 9–11,
  60–1, 121, 152, 179
flocks of birds 117,
  119, 123–6, 141
  how birds fly
    113–14, 122–3
  see also colonies;
  migration
flycatchers 137
food consumption
  64–5, 72, 74
  chicks 16
  during migration
    129, 136–7
fossil birds 1–2
fulmars 80, 153, 154–5

gannets 80, 149, 197
geese 72, 73–4, 90,

126, 137, 172
  flight 123, 126
  and men 91–2, 103,
    108–9, 132–3
gizzards 63
goldcrests 18, 186, 200
golden eagles 115
great auks 180–1
great black-backed gulls
  153
great skuas 149–50, 197
greater spotted wood-
  peckers 42, 200
great tits 16, 39, 193
grebes 19
green woodpeckers 72
greenfinches 42
grey partridges 177
grey wagtails 87
ground dwelling birds
  see flightless birds
grouse 87, 99
guano 88
guillemots 36–7, 197
guinea-fowl 103
gulls 89, 96–7, 150,
  153, 154
  calls 48
  changing habits
    96–7, 106

Haast's eagles 175
hawfinches 160
hawks 77, 99, 168, 170
hearing 75, 78–9
hens 33, 86
  see also chickens
herons 96, 99
herring gulls 106, 150
hobby falcons 92
homosexuality 21–3
honey-buzzards 30
hoopoes 8
house martins 32, 134,
  186

house sparrows 32, 39,
  42, 160, 200–1
hummingbirds 66, 68,
  74, 78, 121
hunting 78–9, 114,
  159–60, 176

Indian hornbills 33–4
instinct 162–72
intelligence 162–72

jays 152, 154

kestrels 159–60
king vultures 81
kingfishers 164
kites 99, 135
kittiwakes 197
kiwis 9–10, 80
kori bustards 11

lapwings 99
larks 54–8, 118–19,
  150, 177
lesser black-backed
  gulls 106
lesser kestrels 141
lesser spotted wood-
  peckers 194
lifespans 16, 38
long-tailed tits 17–18
loons 88
lyrebirds 164

macaws 154
magpies 89, 146–7,
  154, 186
mallard ducks 21
Manx shearwaters 130,
  136, 197
martins 32, 121,
  133–4, 136–7, 171,
  186
mating 13–17, 19–26,
  33–4, 71

migration 64–5, 73,
    127–42, 189, 194–5
    avoiding crossing
        water 135–6
    distance 129–30
    hunting of birds
        during 140–1
    navigation 127–8,
        139, 141–2, 162
    reasons for 131–2
mimicry 164–6, 166–7
moas 179
mockingbirds 164
monogamy 13–14,
    16–17, 23–4
moulting 53, 60, 73–4,
    80–1
mountain quails 130
mute swans 17

nest building 17–18,
    32, 33–4
nightingales 8, 49, 50,
    194
nightjars 159
nostrils 80, 121
nuthatches 42

ospreys 99, 141
ossifrages 99
ostriches 10–11, 63, 76
owls 8, 95, 99, 154
    barn owls 77, 79,
        179–80
    senses 76, 77, 78–9

parakeets 154
parrots 8, 48, 84, 88,
    110
    behaviour 154
    intelligence 163, 164
    lifespan 38
passenger pigeons
    190–1
passerines 48, 74

peacocks 9, 19
pecking order 39
pelicans 9, 67, 96,
    99
penguins 65, 80–1, 121
    emperor 31–2, 60–1,
        121
penises 71–2
peregrine falcons 19,
    193–4
pheasants 20, 120–1,
    190
    eggs 102
    food for 43, 44
    meat 61
pied flycatchers 194
pied wagtails 42
pigeons 102, 107–8,
    151
    food for 43, 44
plantations 199–200
plumage 3, 74, 81,
    114, 150–2
    moulting 53, 60,
        73–4, 80–1
    water birds 71,
        79–80
ptarmigans 189, 199
puffins 34, 68, 149,
    197
purple herons 141

rainforest habitats 187
raising young 16,
    28–37
ravens 6, 89, 99, 172
razorbills 37
red-billed queleas 119
red-wing fieldfares 134
reed buntings 17, 42,
    177
reed warblers 192
respiration 114
robins 15, 46, 142–3,
    144–5

behaviour 151, 154,
    160–1
food for 42, 43
rooks 98, 152
Royal Society for the
    Protection of Birds
    (RSPB) 174, 178
Ruppell's griffon
    vultures 126

sand martins 136–7
sex 15–16, 21–3, 71,
    91
shags 19, 71, 80,
    197
shearwaters 80, 116,
    121, 130, 195–6
siskins 42, 200
skuas 149–50, 197
skylarks 54–8, 177
sleep 69
smell, sense of 80, 81
snow buntings 189
song thrushes 32, 51,
    163, 186
    see also thrushes
sooty shearwaters 130
sooty terns 116
sparrowhawks 30,
    177–8, 186
sparrows 66, 93–4,
    125, 186, 200
    behaviour 150, 151,
        160–1, 163
    human consumption
        of 91, 101, 102
spoonbills 67
spotted flycatchers 194
starlings 98, 104–5, 186
    behaviour 152,
        155–7
    flocks 117, 125
    mimicry 164–5,
        166–7
    nests 32

stone curlews 177
storks 62, 110, 135
storm-petrels 80, 121, 195–6
sunbathing 151
swallows 69, 89, 98, 121, 171
  migration 131, 132, 133, 136, 137
swans 37–8, 96, 99, 147–8
  breeding 16–17, 22
  flight 73–4, 122, 126
swifts 69, 115–16, 121, 133, 171
  migration 134, 136, 137
  nests 100, 116, 139–40
swimming 121, 158

taste, sense of 72
teeth 74
terns 19, 116, 129–30, 154

territory 15, 37, 46, 144–5, 157
thrushes 39, 77, 192–3
  behaviour 151, 160
  song 50, 86
  see also song thrushes
tits 42, 126, 154, 194, 200
  see also blue tits; great tits
toes 74
tongues 72, 74, 75
toucans 82–3
tree sparrows 186
turkey vultures 62, 81, 90–1
turkeys 7, 61, 103
turnstones 66
turtle doves 184

urine 62, 70

vision 75–8, 81
vultures 61–2, 90–1, 99, 126, 198

finding prey 81
flight 121, 135

wall-creepers 130
wandering albatrosses 23–4, 69
warblers 131, 132, 137, 192, 194, 198–9
weather forecasting 135, 171
whitethroats 192
whooper swans 126
willow tits 194
wood pigeons 48, 102
wood warblers 194
woodcocks 77
woodland habitats 194–5
woodlarks 118–19
woodpeckers 65–6, 72, 171, 194, 200
wrens 19, 89, 126, 150
  food for 42, 43

yellowhammers 177

Also by Niall Edworthy

The Curious Gardener's Almanac

The British garden is a living encyclopaedia of curious and fascinating knowledge, the roots of which spread deep into human experience and culture. Gardeners have been growing vegetables, fruit and flowers for centuries. *The Curious Gardener's Almanac* is a collection of remarkable facts, curiosities, ancient wisdom and customs, time-honoured tips, traditional recipes, lists, quotations and general ephemera, celebrating the British garden in all its splendid diversity and rich history. Never dry or dull, the choice of entries in the Almanac is neither categoric nor random: what has found its place here has done so on the merit of its curiosity or genuine use, and nothing else. The topics covered are as profuse and variegated as the world of gardening itself.

Witty and surprising, delve in to *The Curious Gardener's Almanac* and be intrigued, amused, surprised, delighted and inspired.

If you enjoyed this book you may also enjoy
John Lewis-Stempel's

Meadowland
The Private Life of an English Field

'To stand alone in a field in England and listen to the morning chorus of the birds is to remember why life is precious.'

In exquisite prose John Lewis-Stempel records the passing seasons in an ancient meadow on his farm. His unique and intimate account of the birth, life and death of the flora and fauna – from the pair of ravens who have lived there longer than he has to the minutiae underfoot – is threaded throughout with the history of the field and recalls the literature of other observers of our natural history in a remarkable piece of writing that follows the tradition of Jeffries, Mabey and Deakin.

The Running Hare
The Secret Life of Farmland

This is natural history close up and intimate, a closely observed study of the plants and animals that live in and under plough land, from the labouring microbes to the patrolling kestrel above the corn; of field mice in nests woven to crop stems, and the hare now running for his life.

It is a history of the field, which is really the story of our landscape and of us, a people for whom the plough has informed every part of life: our language and religion, our holidays and our food. And it is the story of a field, once moribund and now transformed.

'Indisputably one of the best nature writers of his generation'
COUNTRY LIFE